DATE DUE

Joseph Pulitzer and the New York World

Makers of the Media

Joseph Pulitzer and the New York World

Nancy Whitelaw

MORGAN
REYNOLDS
Incorporated

Greensboro

JOSEPH PULITZER AND THE NEW YORK WORLD

Copyright © 2000 by Nancy Whitelaw

Photo Credits: Library of Congress, New York Historical Society.

Library of Congress Cataloging-in-Publication Data
Whitelaw, Nancy
    Joseph Pulitzer and the New York World / Nancy Whitelaw. —1st ed.
        p.   cm. — (Makers of the Media)
    Includes bibliographical references and index.
    Summary: A biography of the newspaper editor who crusaded against corruption,
established the Pulitzer Prize, and founded the Columbia School of Journalism.
    ISBN   1-883846-44-7
            1. Pulitzer, Joseph, 1847-1911—Juvenile literature. 2. Journalists—United States—
Biography—Juvenile literature. 3. Newspaper publishing—United States—History—
Juvenile literature. [1. Pulitzer, Joseph, 1847-1911— 2. Journalists.]   I. Title II. Series
PN4874. P8W49   1999
070.92—dc21
[B]

                                                                99-14132
                                                                CIP

Printed in the United States of America
First Edition

Dedicated to Patty Baerwald—with love and thanks for introducing me to Conflict Dispute Resolution.

Contents

Joseph Pulitzer

Chapter One

Reporter and Representative

Today complaints about "tabloid journalism" are common. Many blamed Princess Diana's death on tabloid journalism. As she and her companions sped away from pursuing photographers, their car crashed. The Princess was killed, and many argued that the tabloids that would have bought the photos were responsible for her death. The newspapers that can be bought at the check-out line in grocery stores have wild and lurid headlines offering us the "inside scoop" on the personal life of some celebrity or politician. It is not only the tabloids, but all the major media sources, such as "respectable" newspapers and magazines and television news, that are criticized for their never-ending stories of murder, sex scandals, and gossip. This emphasis on the sensational story is said to have led to growing violence and decreasing morality.

This criticism of sensational journalism is not new. In the early years of the United States the popular "penny papers" were criticized for their graphic police reports, stories of mysterious sicknesses and death, articles describing bizarre incidents, and gossip about well-known people.

Joseph Pulitzer, who owned newspapers in the decades after the Civil War, took journalistic sensationalism to new heights. Today he is often referred to as the father of modern "tabloid journalism." The *New York World* and other Pulitzer papers published articles and editorials exposing fraud in politics and business. They also printed stories about crime, sex, and weird events. Pulitzer knew that these types of stories would increase circulation and make him a wealthy man.

Today the most prestigious prize in American journalism is named after Joseph Pulitzer. The Pulitzer Prize is awarded from the Journalism School at Columbia University that he funded. It has been said that Pulitzer gave this money to make amends for the type of journalism that made him rich. There is no way to know if this is true. But what is true is that Joseph Pulitzer made a powerful impact on the way newspapers operate in the United States and other parts of the world. It is also true that his life story is a fascinating example of the American success story—and a reminder that immense wealth can not always bring one happiness.

Young Joseph Pulitzer wanted control over his life, himself, and everyone he met. So when his widowed mother married a man he did not like, sixteen-year-old Joseph decided to leave his home in Budapest, Hungary. It was 1863, and Joseph planned to enroll in the Austrian Army. The recruiters told him to go back home. They said he was too young, his vision was poor, and he was too thin.

He decided to go to Paris. There he applied to the French foreign legion, hoping to be sent to Mexico to help Louis Napoleon. The recruiters told him to go back home. He heard the same story about his age, his vision, and his physique.

Maybe he would find a solution in London. There he tried to enlist in the British army, hoping to be sent to India to fight for the English. He was rejected with the same story as in Austria and France.

He went on to Hamburg, Germany. He applied to become a sailor on one of the many ships traveling in and out of this busy seaport. Again, the answer was no.

In the summer of 1864, Joseph Pulitzer met an agent looking for soldiers for the Union Army in America's Civil War. The agent didn't care about age or vision or body condition. All he cared about was the bounty he would earn for each volunteer he brought back. It didn't take long for Joseph to get on the ship headed across the Atlantic.

It didn't take him long to make another decision, either. He decided that he would collect the bounty for himself instead of letting the agent collect it. Almost before the ship was anchored in Boston harbor, he dove off the deck and swam to shore. Quickly, in order to avoid arrest, he hopped on a train to New York. There he found lots of recruiting booths with officers eager to sign him up and give him his bounty. By September 30, he was a member of the Lincoln Cavalry of the Union Army of the United States of America. Most of the recruits were German, so language was hardly a problem for him.

He was assigned to a camp in Maryland. There he didn't fool anyone when he said that he was eighteen. The commanding officer took one look at him and said "Take that little ----- away from here! I don't want him in my company." He was shifted to another company, and again harassed because of his age and his Jewish background. He lost control. He hit one of his tormentors. Luckily for him, a captain saved him from punishment. But the teasing did not stop, and he had few friends.

The company had to wait, bored and restless, until they received orders to move on. When these orders finally came, Joseph was little better off than before. His regiment was kept busy with a lot of riding and some minor skirmishes. He still did not like his comrades, and he hated the army food. Most of all he hated the army regulations that kept him from having any control over his life.

After the Confederate surrender in 1865, the seventeen-year-old veteran took his mustering out—or discharge—pay and gladly left military service. He was away from the control of the military, but far from in control of his own life. He was just one of thousands of young ex-soldiers suddenly without an occupation, and with no job skills. He had received a fine private education in Budapest, but his experience with European arts and letters did not prepare him for a career. Here he was simply another immigrant who spoke only broken English.

With just thirteen dollars in his pocket, he left for New Bedford, Massachusetts, hoping to get a job on a whaling ship. But he was out of luck. The war had disrupted the once-profitable industry, and there were no jobs. So he went back to New York to look for work. But as a foreigner with no job skills, he found nothing. Somebody suggested that he go to St. Louis, Missouri, where jobs were supposed to be more plentiful.

That might have been a good idea for some young men. But Joseph had no money, no food, and no transportation. He sold his only possession, a silk handkerchief, to buy a little food. For transportation he traveled in freight cars, changing cars frequently to avoid being caught. After days on the trains, he saw city lights in the dimness ahead. Hoping that these were the lights of St. Louis, he hopped off the train. He was right about the city lights but wrong about the place to get off the train. Between him and the city were the cold and dark, and the Mississippi River too wide to swim across at that place. A ferry was available, but Joseph had no money for that.

He asked for a job in return for passage on the ferry. The captain asked if he could stoke the coal fire. Of course, answered Joseph. He shoveled coal into the large boiler for several trips across the river on a cold and rainy night while the captain ridiculed him for his heavy accent.

Once he arrived in the city, he searched through the want ads in the German-language paper, the *Westliche Post*. The job that most appealed to him was keeper of mules. He walked four miles to Benton Barracks to apply, and he accepted the job of caretaker of sixteen mules. But there were a couple of problems he had no control over. The animals were more stubborn than he had imagined, and he could not stand the food that was part of his pay. After just two days on the job, he went back to the ferry master and got a job operating the gates.

He didn't like that job either. So he found odd jobs on a river steamer headed for Memphis, Tennessee. He might have stayed there for a while, but an epidemic of cholera scared him away. He went back to St. Louis and joined a crew of workers unloading steamers. Then he worked for the same company checking in deliveries. After a while, he became supervisor of a small group of workers. But he was far from satisfied with his life.

He took a job as waiter in a local restaurant. But his temper got the better of him. When he became angry with a customer, he dumped a plate of steak on his head. He was thrown out of the restaurant. Although he worked at a few odd jobs, he soon used up his wages from the restaurant. He slept in the streets and picked up food wherever he could. For a while he worked for the Department of Health, helping record their fight against an epidemic of cholera. He was valuable in the department because he could speak with the many German immigrants who needed medical help. But one day a fellow worker was awarded a promotion that Joseph had expected for himself. Joseph lost his temper and quit.

One of his longest-running jobs was for a lawyer who was securing rights for construction of a railroad that would run from St. Louis to San Francisco, California. Joseph's job was to secure charters for the land in twelve counties. He learned many basic survival skills as he surveyed this mostly uninhabited land. He managed to escape the fate of one of his co-workers who drowned in an attempt to ford a river at flood-stage. His employers praised his enthusiasm, courage, and accuracy. They encouraged him to become a lawyer. In most states, the only requirement to become a lawyer was to have "good moral character."

When Joseph was laid off because he was no longer needed, he remembered this suggestion. He found a positive side to unemployment. With time on his hands, he spent hours in the Mercantile Library where he read and read, never satisfying his appetite for books about many different subjects. Because of the large German population in the city, he found plenty of books in German, and he improved his understanding of English by reading books in English.

Some mornings he could hardly wait for the library to open. When the librarians arrived to open the doors, they found him waiting on the steps. He read until lunchtime, ate a couple of apples, and then went back to the books. He left at closing time just before the librarians did. He may have strained his already weak eyes by so much reading, but he would not let that stop him.

Some days he interrupted his reading to take a job as messenger and errand boy. Sometimes he earned enough money to rent a room for a while. When he had this luxury, he often read far into the night, squinting in the dim gaslight. Studying for the bar was no problem for Joseph. He used the library for his classroom. Like former President Abraham Lincoln, Pulitzer prepared for the law almost entirely by self-directed reading.

In March 1867, twenty-year-old Joseph decided that his future lay in America. He became an American citizen. Then he became a notary public. Then he applied for and received admission to the bar. Very little is recorded about his activities as a lawyer. Perhaps his youth and his strong accent discouraged potential clients.

He continued to seek other jobs and to spend time in the library. While in the reading room, he became friends with a high school instructor with whom he played chess. This man introduced him to other German-speaking residents of St. Louis. Through these contacts, he obtained a part-time job helping German immigrants adjust to living in the St. Louis area. Slowly but surely, Joseph Pulitzer was acquiring a reputation for being industrious, responsible, and helpful.

In 1868, he applied for a job as reporter for the German-language newspaper *Westliche Post*. He got the job. "I could not believe it," he said. "I, the unknown, the luckless, almost a boy of the streets, selected for such a responsibility. It all seemed like a dream." He often worked from ten a.m. until two o'clock the next morning, putting more strain on his already weak eyes as he read and wrote in poor light in the evening and early morning hours. He stopped at nothing in his eagerness to excel in his new job. Some of his co-workers made fun of his enthusiasm and high energy. They laughed at the tall gaunt figure with the tiny red beard who bounced into the office each day, eager to take on every possible task. This teasing didn't bother him much. He had matured since he was the butt of jokes in the military, and he now had better control over his temper.

He gave suggestions for columns, wrote articles, and worked with editorials. Readers appreciated the way he focused on accuracy. With Joseph as reporter, the *Westliche Post* became popular. A reporter on a competing newspaper said of him, "He was quick, intelligent and enthusiastic, but of all his qualities the most notable was his determination to accomplish whatever he set out to do."

Soon the city of St. Louis and the state of Missouri recognized the name of Joseph Pulitzer the journalist. Some politicians and other community leaders asked for his advice and support. Some English-language newspapers translated his articles for their own pages. Citizens of St. Louis became fond of this young gentleman who showed up at many important civic, social, and cultural events. He became more interested in politics.

The paper honored his request to attend the Republican state convention in December 1869. His assignment was to write an article about the nomination of a candidate for the legislature. There was no candidate. While he was out of the meeting room for a minute, his fellow reporters decided that he should be the representative. He objected. He was not American-born, and even if he was, he was not old enough under the rules. Besides, he didn't know anything about the position. The committee nominated him anyway. He accepted, put his heart and soul into a campaign, and defeated his Democratic opponent by a vote of 209 to 147. After the election, he attended the legislature both as a reporter and as a representative. Some of the representatives claimed that Representative Pulitzer had an unfair advantage as Reporter Pulitzer.

He said that was no problem for him. With both titles, he had roughly the same job--to fight for honesty and justice. And he was eager to fight. He had seen the deplorable conditions in the county-run poorhouse and insane asylum, and he wanted them changed immediately. So he drafted a bill to reform the County Court that supervised these human services. To add punch to his bill, he questioned the motives of Captain Edward Augustine, a county official.

Later, he met Augustine at a political gathering at a hotel. Augustine called Joseph a liar. Joseph left the room and returned a few minutes later with a pistol. The two men argued again. Then Joseph pulled out his gun. Just before the bullet left the barrel, Augustine rushed at Joseph and knocked him down. The bullet struck Augustine in the leg, inflicting a minor wound.

Joseph was arrested for assault. Influential friends helped him to get off with a hundred dollar fine for breaching the peace. Joseph declared himself a winner in the fight against fraud and dedicated himself to routing out corruption wherever he could find it.

There was a lot of corruption to be found all the way from the highest officials in the country down to petty crooks. The election of President Ulysses S. Grant in 1868 brought an era of scandal in the finance markets, accusations of bribe taking among high officials, and the selling of jobs by government department heads. In his writing for the *Westliche Post*, Joseph carried on a continuous campaign against fraud at every level. Language was no problem for

Joseph Pulitzer, age twenty-one, when he worked as a reporter for the *Westliche Post.*

him; he thought in German and then quickly translated his ideas into English.

His strong writing and firm views brought Joseph to the attention of Governor Benjamin B. Brown, who appointed him one of three police commissioners in St. Louis. Twenty-four-year-old Joseph accepted the two-year appointment with both hope and joy. He fought tirelessly against the gambling commissions. Sometimes assaulted, often verbally attacked, Joseph continued his campaigns, building an ever-stronger reputation as a person who feared no man or organization in his fight for truth and justice.

Joseph was elected a delegate to the Liberal Republican Party convention held in early 1872. He quickly rose to secretary of that organization and made sixty speeches urging the nomination of journalist Horace Greeley for president. Greeley supported temperance, women's rights, and a system of socialist communities among other issues.

Editors at the *Westliche Post,* frustrated by the political climate, offered Joseph a controlling interest in the paper. The twenty-five-year-old writer jumped at the chance. He bought the shares on credit, and with new self-confidence, he moved to a splendid hotel. He campaigned even more earnestly for Greeley, making over sixty speeches for him. He put in more time on the paper, hoping that it would gain in prestige when Greeley won the presidency.

That November, Greeley gathered fewer than three million votes and lost the election to Grant. Joseph's spirits fell. All his work had not helped Greeley, the paper, or himself. He dropped his membership in the Republican Party. He sold his interest in the paper for $30,000, enough so he had cash left over, and left for a vacation in Europe and Hungary.

His trip did not revive his spirits. He was not looking for fun and relaxation; he was looking for control over his life. Back in New York, an offer to buy a German daily paper, the *Staats Zeitung,* seemed to be the answer. He worked with the failing paper for just a short while. When he realized that this was no answer, he sold it for twenty thousand dollars and sold the machinery to a newly established newspaper. Now he had money. He threw his career questions to the wind and enjoyed a social life of riding, operas, balls, and parties.

Then he was bitten again by the political bug. As the country worked at restoration after the Civil War, questions about states' rights took center front. On one side were the citizens who believed that each state had the right to make its own laws, independent of the federal government. On the other side, citizens believed that each state should yield to the federal government when conflict arose. Leaders scheduled a Constitutional Convention to discuss these problems. Joseph got himself elected a delegate to the convention to be held in May 1875.

He spoke strongly and often at that meeting. He focused on the importance of a strong national government and on the rights of individuals. He also spoke for the broadest possible education and for strong public schools. He added that he would like to see government paying more attention to education and less to punishment for ignorance of laws.

The convention excited him, but left him no better off than before. He still had no job. However, he did have a strong desire to work in journalism. His career goal was to be in control of a newspaper. So he looked for a paper to buy. He didn't find one in America, so he went to Europe to find one. He was disappointed there, too.

Chapter Two

From Reporter to Publisher

Back in America in 1876, Pulitzer jumped into politics again. He made a lot of speeches in favor of presidential candidate Samuel Tilden, a Democrat who was running against Republican Rutherford Hayes. By now, his command of English was impressive. He reasoned well, and he had the kind of voice and language necessary to be a good speechmaker. Audiences applauded his ideas designed to smooth over the hatreds created by the Civil War: "We are one people, one country and one government." Perhaps he was too inspiring for his own good. Before election day, he had developed weak lungs and sometimes he spit up blood. The presidential vote was so close that the outcome had to be decided by the Electoral Commission some time after the vote.

Owners of the *New York Sun* hired Joseph as a reporter with the assignment to cover the process of the Electoral Commission. This assignment won for Joseph a seldom-granted privilege—he was allowed to sign his articles.

But this deep and successful involvement in journalism was not enough for thirty-year-old Joseph. He had fallen in love with Kate Davis, a beautiful young woman, and a member of Washington's high society. What could he offer her? The status of wife of a reporter did not fit in with her family's social standards. A lawyer might meet these standards, but Joseph had no interest in the practice. Making his situation more difficult, he spoke with a guttural accent. Probably the deepest difficulty lay in his heritage. Joseph's father was a Jew, and Jews were not accepted into the social and business world of Washington. Joseph was also aware of a personal weakness. He was frequently a victim of emotions that plunged him into despair. He had suffered from this handicap frequently--when his favored candidate lost a political race or he failed to complete negotiations to buy a paper or when someone challenged his views publicly.

Still, he would not give up the idea of marrying Kate. He wrote to her: "I cannot help saying that I am not worthy of such love, I am too cold and selfish, I know."

Determined to grasp control of this situation, he asked to become a partner in the German or English edition of the popular magazine *Puck*. With this position, he could keep alive his dreams of working in publishing while he remained close enough to Kate to continue his courtship. The editor turned him down. Then he heard what he had heard eleven years earlier when he was adjusting to civilian life: go to St. Louis where opportunities await. He left Washington after writing to Kate that he needed to "become worthy of you, worthy of your faith and love, worthy of a better and finer future."

Apparently he did become worthy. Kate agreed to marry him in 1878. They planned a ten-week honeymoon in Europe after a June wedding. He wrote frequently to Kate and asked that she do the same: "Write me every day, my child, and not so briefly." With comments like this, he established the hierarchy in the marriage: she was an adorable child, and he was the loving parent who would discipline as he thought necessary.

When they arrived in Europe, Kate learned that her new husband had planned more than a honeymoon. He had a contract to write articles for the *Sun*. He wrote studies of the political situation in France and Germany, warning that a war between France and

Germany seemed inevitable. He had other newspaper business on his mind as well. He hoped to buy a European newspaper. These negotiations failed.

Back in America in early September, Pulitzer received a little payment for his articles for the *Sun*. This money was not enough to live on for very long. It seemed that he could not buy a newspaper. He could not even get the kind of job he respected as a reporter. So he decided to try his luck in St. Louis again—this time as a lawyer. Kate stayed in Washington, and he traveled west.

One of the first pieces of news he learned in St. Louis was that the *St. Louis Dispatch* was bankrupt. It would be auctioned off to the highest bidder. The *Dispatch* was not the paper that Pulitzer had dreamed of owning. The circulation was less than two thousand. The office building was dilapidated, and the press machinery was old and needed constant repair. But it was a newspaper, and it could be his. Without a backward glance at a law practice, he decided that he would spend all he had if necessary—a little over $5,000—to buy the paper.

On a cold and windy day in December, Pulitzer stood on the courthouse steps with others interested in the auction. He had asked his friend Simon Arnold to do the bidding for him. Pulitzer simply stood and watched. The first bid was $1,000. Arnold joined the competition. The bids rose. Arnold bid $2,500. The bidding stopped. After a pause, the auctioneer announced that Arnold's bid completed the sale. Pulitzer owned a newspaper.

This was December 9. Pulitzer was determined to get out an issue on December 10. He found a few *Dispatch* workers who had remained faithful to the failing business. They agreed to put together enough copy to complete an issue. After they completed the dummy--the preliminary mockup of the newspaper—they faced their most difficult problem. The pressroom was several floors below them, and the elevator was broken. They solved the problem by sliding the copy down the stairs to pressmen waiting there to gather it up. By noon

Although Pulitzer did not think he was worthy of marrying Kate Davis, the couple honeymooned in Europe after marrying in 1878.

one thousand copies of Pulitzer's *Dispatch* were on the newsstands.

The next day the editor of the *St. Louis Post* recognized the threat of competition from the *Dispatch*. He offered Pulitzer a deal in which the two papers would merge. Pulitzer's answer was "Yes." Just three days after he bought the *Dispatch*, Pulitzer became a partner in the *Post-Dispatch*. Proudly he announced the merger in the new paper: "The *Post and Dispatch* will serve no party but the people; will be no organ of Republicanism, but the organ of truth will not support the 'Administration', but criticize it."

He had much to learn in this new venture. He knew something about reporting, but he did not know about news gathering, headlines, layout, circulation, operation of machines, supervision of employees, business procedures or bookkeeping. Besides these challenges, he set two goals. One was to increase circulation, and to do it quickly. The other was to become an agent for reform. He proclaimed himself a fighter in one of his first editorials: "What is the great demoralizer of our public life? Of cour se, corruption. And what causes corruption? Of course, the greed for money."

He attacked the tax system as an example of greed. In editorials, he described how the system worked to shield the rich from paying taxes. He might have chosen an easier fight for his first appearance as editor of the *Post-Dispatch*. Many wealthy people who paid little in taxes advertised in his paper. Could he afford to offend them? Yes, he could. And he did. He published column after column naming people who reported to the tax system that they had few or no assets. Most citizens of St. Louis knew that these people lived in mansions, rode in fancy carriages, and wore elegant clothes to their frequent parties. Pulitzer both lost and won in this crusade. He lost some advertisers and supporters. He won respect for his paper.

Pulitzer knew that a single crusade would boost circulation for a short time only. In order to build a dependable readership, he needed to have a new reform movement every week or every month. He

Joseph Pulitzer when he was the publisher of the *St. Louis Post-Dispatch*.

created crusades to attack a lottery, a horse-car monopoly, and insurance fraud. He knew that powerful headlines would attract readers, but not for long unless the inside pages followed up on the stories promised on the front page. He worked from early morning late into the night, pushing his staff to keep up with him. Articles about crimes, scandals, and possible fraud came pouring off the presses. Headlines promised a list of owners of prostitution houses. A front-page story gave details of a well-known heiress who married without her parents' permission. Another article quoted from a letter written by an army officer just before he committed suicide. After a front-page report on problems with a committee named by the governor, two of the members resigned. As a direct result of *Post-Dispatch* articles, members of a gambling ring were arrested, fined, and imprisoned.

Sensationalist! That accusation against Pulitzer rang loud and clear, especially from those who had something to lose from Pulitzer's reform movement. Nonsense, he replied. Far from being a sensationalist, he was a down-to-earth publisher who worked with facts, not exaggeration. And look at the good he did, he said. A person tempted to do something wrong would think twice if he knew it might be reported in a newspaper. Besides, the *Post-Dispatch* also supported civic improvement. *Post-Dispatch* editorials called for cleaning and repairing of streets, a new exposition building to bring tourists into the city, and a system of parks.

When Ralph Pulitzer was born in June 1879, Pulitzer vowed to take Sundays off to be with his growing family. Kate appreciated this, but she had concerns about her husband's safety. She was well aware of the passions roused by Pulitzer, and she was afraid that someone who considered the paper an enemy might attack him. He often worked at the office until midnight or later.

His partner grew tired of being dominated by this tireless man. He sold his share of the paper to Pulitzer for $40,000. Immediately,

Pulitzer named himself president of the paper.

The *Post-Dispatch* continued to swamp the competition. By the end of 1879, the *Star* had gone out of business. The *Post-Dispatch*, now the only English-language evening newspaper in the city, reached a circulation of five thousand. Advertising doubled the size of the paper to eight pages. Pulitzer hired John Cockerill, a well-known journalist, as editor. In hiring Cockerill, he hoped to free himself up to campaign in advance of the fall elections.

Pulitzer's conversation focused on issues, candidates, and political strategies. He became a bore to friends and family who could not get him to talk of anything else. Sometimes his excitement about candidates left him sleepless at night and irritable during the day. When his favored candidate seemed to be losing, he became depressed. He created a goal for himself. He could not become president because he was foreign-born, "but some day I am going to elect a president." With this goal in mind, he won a seat at the state Democratic convention. Then he ran in the Democratic primary for congressional representative. He lost by 700 to 4,200 votes—a victim of a corrupt political machine. Pulitzer was devastated. "I am out of public life," he declared.

Lucille Irma Pulitzer was born in September of 1880. Pulitzer stayed home about a week to meet his new daughter. Then he went to work supporting the Democratic Party's presidential nominee, Winfield Scott Hancock. In November, Hancock lost to James Garfield, the Republican candidate.

Pulitzer went back to work full-time on the paper. By December 1880, circulation was almost 9,000, and he ended the year with an annual profit of over $40,000. Pulitzer was a rich man.

The keys to his success had been reform and sensational news. He continued with these focuses. When his reporters could not find attention-getting stories, Pulitzer helped to create them. He attacked variety shows, prostitution, abortion, and opium, and he advertised his attacks with headlines like "An Adulterous Pair," "Duped and Deserted," "Kissing in Church." He was sued several times for libel, but his accusers could not make the charges stick. Some said that his sensational stories were motivated by his greed to make money-selling papers. He said that all his stories were motivated by his search for drama in life.

By December 1881, the *Post-Dispatch* had outgrown its old and run-down offices. Pulitzer used some of the $85,000 annual profit to construct a new building and to equip it with efficient machinery, including two modern presses. He used some of the money to make his reporters the highest-paid in the city. He gave generous rewards to workers who were especially industrious, including some news-boys to whom he gave watches and clothes.

Pulitzer now had all the money he wanted and high standing in the community. But his health was not good. He suffered from nervousness, insomnia, and weakening vision. His doctors said that if he continued to work and to worry for twelve to sixteen hours a day, he would become more nervous, sleepless, and perhaps lose his sight. He forced himself to take short vacations to New York where he could visit his brother, Albert. But he didn't leave his business concerns in St. Louis. He spent lots of time talking about the newspaper business with Albert, who was considering starting his own paper. Also, Pulitzer always had an eye out for another news-paper to buy.

In June 1882, Katherine Ethel Pulitzer was born. That fall, neither Ralph nor his father was well. The family spent the winter in Aiken, (Aachen) Germany, near the French border. While he was away, his managing editor Cockerill was accused of murdering a lawyer during a political argument. In court, the judge ruled that no charges would be filed. But popular opinion ran against Cockerill, and readership of the *Post-Dispatch* dropped. On one hand, Pulitzer wanted to stand behind his editor and friend. On the other hand, he would not accept a loss in circulation. When circulation decreased by thirteen hundred papers in just a few weeks, Pulitzer fired Cockerill. He chose his former partner, John Dillon, to succeed him.

Circulation continued to drop. By winter it was down by another thousand. Pulitzer lost faith in his ability to succeed in St. Louis. Poor health weakened his body; despair weakened his spirit. In the spring of 1883, he agreed to follow his doctor's orders to take a complete rest.

He decided to spend the time in Europe. But something happened in New York before he boarded the ship.

Chapter Three

The *World* in His Hands

Pulitzer spent a few days with his brother Albert, now publisher of the *New York Morning Journal*. They discussed the stories they had heard about a failing paper, the twenty-year-old *World*. The *World* had started as a one-penny religious newspaper. When that venture failed financially, it merged with another paper and became *The World and Courier and Enquirer*, a paper that supported the Democratic Party. During the Civil War, its editor was arrested for misrepresenting President Abraham Lincoln. Next, a railroad president who had no experience in journalism bought the paper. When that venture failed, the paper was sold to Jay Gould, a wealthy investor. Under Gould, the paper featured excellent writers, but readership did not grow. The Pulitzer brothers listened to the rumors and wondered if it were true that the *World* was for sale again.

Pulitzer's plans for a vacation evaporated. His plans to buy the *World* became a priority. Pulitzer hoped he had the money, he knew he had the ambition, and he believed he had the ability to run the *World*. This might be his chance to work toward his three long-held goals.

One of his goals was to elect a president. The presidential election would take place the following year. Another goal was to sell millions of newspapers. His third goal was to lead reform to make the life of the common person more satisfying. He believed that he could accomplish these three goals if he controlled a major newspaper. He was determined that nervous depression, insomnia, or fear of losing his vision would not stop him.

Six-foot-two, with a full, reddish beard, Pulitzer was the picture of health as he arrived at the offices of the *World*. He stepped quickly and confidently out of his carriage and into the Western Union Building on Broadway. He had an appointment with Jay Gould, owner of the *World*.

Both men were shrewd bargainers. Gould knew that Pulitzer had wanted to buy another paper for many years. Pulitzer knew that the paper was losing about $40,000 a year and had a circulation of only about fifteen thousand. Gould stated his price—over a half million dollars. He added two conditions: Pulitzer must buy the *World* building at an additional $200,000, and he must promise to keep most of the *World* staff in their jobs.

The bargaining process overwhelmed Pulitzer. Against his will, nervousness, depression, and fear overcame him. He could not cope with the unanswerable questions. What about the competition from the *Herald*, the *Sun,* the *Times*, the *Tribune*, the *Star*, the *Truth*, and his own brother's *Morning Journal?* Was he strong enough physically and emotionally to accept the responsibility for a failing newspaper? Was his brother right in his belief that New Yorkers would not accept two Pulitzer-run papers?

He told Kate that he was no longer interested in the paper. She told him that he was listening to emotion, not reason. She persuaded him to continue negotiations with Gould.

On April 28, Pulitzer concluded the deal. He would pay almost $350,000 in installments with the debt to be paid in full by 1886. He leased, rather than bought, the building. He retained the right to select his own staff. He wrote to a friend: "If there is anything in my melancholy life's work which I hope and wish may do good, it is that it should give encouragement to thousands of hardworking journalists who honestly believe that they have no chance of ever becoming owners or partners of newspapers "

The two-cent paper was eight pages, with six columns on each page. The heading showed the words *The World* with icons of two globes, each radiating rays of light.

He started right off on his goal of making life more satisfying for the common person. New York City was a perfect place to carry on a crusade for reform. Corruption and fraud dominated government, fueled by political machines like Tammany Hall, an arm of the Democratic Party. Tammany gave out jobs and contracts in return for votes and money. Streets were dirty, decent housing did not exist, and schools and other public institutions suffered. Half a million immigrants poured into the country each year, and many remained in New York where they docked. Exploitation of the poor increased with each new wave of immigrants. As penniless men and women entered the workplace, wages dropped to $1.25 for a man who worked 10-12 hours a day; women and children earned about fifty cents a day. Most lived in a slum called the Bowery, in the harbor area, or in dilapidated housing or in another section of the city.

Pulitzer wanted the *World* to be a paper for the exploited as well as for those who were better off. He told his reporters that they were now writing for an audience of desperately poor people. He said, "Heretofore you have all been living in the parlour and taking baths every day. Now I wish you to understand that, in future, you are all walking down the Bowery."

Besides helping the common person, Pulitzer was working on his goal of selling millions of newspapers. Immigrants needed information about housing, jobs, and other aspects of their new lives. The *World* would speak to and for these people. Pulitzer was not aiming at a group of readers to be snatched from a competing newspaper. One out of every five Americans could neither read nor write. Thousands of others were barely literate. Pulitzer told his reporters

Pulitzer bought the *New York World* from Jay Gould, one of the most notorious businessmen of the era.

to keep these people in mind as they chose and wrote stories.

First of all, they should use short headlines, simple sentences, and informal vocabulary. He wanted stories about lower-class people who were especially hard working, courageous, or successful. He also wanted gossip about the higher classes since such articles would attract readers of all classes. He wanted stories of sex, crime, and tragedy. No more dull headlines about the economy or the political situation in Albany. One first page of Pulitzer's *World* told about a hula dancer. Another focused on a condemned killer demanding his release from jail. Another told of a burglar arrested on his wedding day.

He was revolutionary in his use of photos and illustrations in the paper. The first newspaper illustration—that of a volcano—appeared in 1638 in England. In 1754, Benjamin Franklin printed a woodcut of a snake symbolizing independence in the *Pennsylvania Gazette*. Now Pulitzer urged his editors to use photos and illustrations to a greater extent than had been done before. One well-received illustration was a four-column wide drawing of the newly opened Brooklyn Bridge. Diagrams of murders and other crimes were popular. The newspaper published photos of the poor at Christmas without any food, the horrors of the lack of sanitation in the tenements, and weary horse-car drivers forced to work more than twelve hours a day.

In his zeal to uproot corruption, he published a list of ten goals necessary to achieve social justice. These included higher taxes for the wealthy, reforming the civil service, punishing corrupt government officials, and safeguarding elections against fraud.

Pulitzer was leading a revolution in the newspaper business. The mix of politics, social reform, and sensational and gossipy articles brought many faithful readers to the *World*.

In his dedication to make society a better place, he determined to make the newspaper as perfect as possible. He bounced in and out of staff offices shouting at writers: cut the wordiness out of their articles, tantalize readers with intriguing subjects, use strong verbs, always be accurate. Since he could not be everywhere at once-- although some workers thought he tried to be—he sometimes hired two men to do approximately the same job. He reasoned that each man would work especially hard because he would feel competitive with the other man. Not all his workers agreed with this. One writer wrote that this competition squelched cooperation: "If you had asked a man a question he looked at you as though you were trying to take something away from him."

Working on his goal of electing a president, Pulitzer was a man in a hurry. He wanted to establish a strong relationship between the paper and its readers in time to influence the 1884 elections. Some of his work centered on the 5,000,000 immigrants who had entered the country in the last ten years. To a large degree, politicians neglected them. Pulitzer knew how to appeal to them by pointing out the fraud and corruption that kept them from participating in the flourishing economy. These people could become the soldiers in Pulitzer's election battles if only he could convince them to read and trust the paper.

Every day the pages of the *World* reminded readers of the elegant castle-like homes of the newest millionaires just blocks away from the dirty unlit rooms and open sewers of the slums. Editorials blasted Tammany Hall for offering city jobs in return for votes. Pulitzer wrote an editorial scolding the wealthiest citizens for frivolously using their wealth. He waged a campaign against contrived bank failures that robbed people of their savings. He knew that many would-be readers were simply not interested in politics. He hoped to change that attitude by attracting them to read the paper for other interests, hoping their eyes would stray to the more serious articles.

He was devastated when two-year-old Katherine died of pneumonia in the spring of 1884. He tried to work out his grief by spending even more time at the newspaper.

To attract male readers, he published a long editorial praising sports and the value of physical competition. He printed schedules of sporting events—baseball, horse racing, track, tennis, football. One-half of his potential readers were women, and many of these women were pushing at the limits placed on them by society. For them, he created an advice column where fictional "Edith" wrote to her country cousin Bessie, giving her advice on how to be socially proper when she moved to the city. Edith included topics like how to give a dinner party, how to give a tea, and how to act at a ball. The column was widely popular. Upper-class women read it to check out their social awareness. Lower-class women read it to fantasize about the wealthy. And men of all classes read it out of curiosity. Another woman's column was written by "Jenny June" who told women that they could take their rightful places in the community if they would only try harder.

To attract Sunday readers, he faced another problem. Tradition dictated that no one should engage in entertainment on the Sabbath. Pulitzer knew that many of his readers were laborers who worked sixteen hours a day, six days a week. He believed that they deserved rest and relaxation on Sunday. He created for them a Sunday paper that was entertaining. He featured articles about topics like cannibalism, life in prison, human sacrifice, and other unusual subjects. Sunday circulation rose steadily from 15,000 when Pulitzer bought the *World* to 39,000.

Chapter Four

A French Goddess

When the Democratic Party asked Pulitzer to run for Congress in the ninth district of New York, he accepted. Although outwardly he showed little enthusiasm, he was delighted to have the opportunity. Since the district was safely Democratic, he spent very little time campaigning.

In the fall, he expanded the paper to ten pages daily and twelve on Sunday. Other papers, facing competition from the two-cent *World,* dropped their prices, some from four cents to three and others from three cents to two. Still, the *World* held its lead in circulation.

Now was the time for Pulitzer to fulfill his goal to get a president elected. He chose Democrat Grover Cleveland, governor of New York, as his candidate. He gave four reasons why Cleveland should be elected: (1) "he is an honest man," (2) "he is an honest man," (3) "he is an honest man," (4) "he is an honest man."

Cleveland was running against Republican James Blaine. Each man had sex problems that tarnished his candidacy. Cleveland was known to be the father of an illegitimate child; Blaine married the mother of his child just three months before that baby was born. Throughout September and October, the race was too close to call. Then on October 29, Blaine held a fund-raising dinner for two hundred wealthy Republicans. He spoke to the group about Republican prosperity. Pulitzer attacked him ferociously in the editorial pages of the *World*. He asked how a candidate for president could talk about prosperity when so many were unemployed, homeless, and hungry. The editorial attracted a lot of attention.

The final count gave Cleveland a margin of only 25,000 votes out of a total of almost ten million cast. Pulitzer took credit for the victory, and many of his readers agreed that the *World* editorials had made the difference for Cleveland. In that same election, Pulitzer won a seat in Congress by 15,000 to 8,000 votes.

Joseph Pulitzer had invented a modern newspaper with a style that other newspapers soon copied. He attracted thousands of readers of all classes with his stories on reform, personal strengths and weaknesses, and entertainment. Most important to him, he used the newspaper as a political force. The staff of the *World* was recognized as the best in the country, and aspiring journalists could reach no higher than a goal of writing for Pulitzer's paper. Two years after Pulitzer bought the *World*, the paper was the most widely read daily in the western hemisphere.

Some competitors complained that Pulitzer attracted readers by reporting on stories about violence, sex, and crimes. He answered: "Let those who are startled by it blame the people who are before the mirror, and not the mirror, which only reflects their features and their actions." He said that he did a service to his readers by making them aware of corruption and crime and exposing the guilty. The paper only described crimes; it did not create them.

An example of strong attention-getting writing came in a series of articles about businessman William Vanderbilt, who was believed to possess about $200 million. The newspaper pointed out that Vanderbilt paid no income taxes because he reported that his debts exceeded his income. Look at his wealth, said the *World*. If all his money were in gold bricks, the bricks would weigh 350 tons. If Vanderbilt wanted to move his wealth, he would need twenty-five freight cars or seventy elephants. Readers laughed at first, then

Pulitzer worked hard to keep James Blaine from being elected president of the United States.

became angry. Their anger turned against the tax system and the politicians who administered it. This is exactly the result Pulitzer had hoped for.

The paper prospered, and Pulitzer shared with his employees. He gave rewards to enterprising reporters and editors, and he handed out turkeys at Thanksgiving and Christmas.

When Pulitzer attended his first congressional meeting, he was determined to wipe out high taxes that benefited only the wealthy. But he soon was consumed with what he considered petty politics— never-ending requests for a job or office, a debate about the manufacture of oleomargarine, pleas from the Temperance Society. The more Pulitzer learned about the slow and inefficient workings of Congress, the more frustrated he became. As usual, when his frustration rose, his health suffered.

From the time he bought the paper, he had over-exerted himself and still always felt that he should have done more. Leaving the office to go to Washington increased his frustration with himself.

The two jobs together were more than he could take. All he could think of was that he needed a long rest in Europe. After rest and relaxation there, he planned to reconsider his priorities. He would not set a sailing date until after his fourth child was born in early spring. Joseph Pulitzer II arrived in March. But Pulitzer did not sail immediately. His attention was caught by a national problem more important to him than rest and relaxation.

The situation concerned a gift from France to America. The French government had commissioned the sculpture of a goddess to stand in the New York harbor holding a torch of freedom. The statue would signify the strong bond between the two countries.

At first, the two countries worked together. The French government commissioned Auguste Bartholdi to design the statue. The American government declared that Bedloe's Island, later renamed Liberty Island, in the harbor would be the setting. Americans established a committee to raise funds for the pedestal that would lift the statue one hundred feet above sea level. In April 1883, French workers were ready to pack pieces of the 145-foot tall statue into boxes for shipping, but American citizens had not yet done their part. There was no base, and there were no funds to build one. The statue stayed in France.

Now in 1885, Pulitzer thought again of his arrival in New York twenty-one years earlier. He remembered the thrill of first seeing the land of promise. He loved the idea of a welcoming statue in the harbor. He ignored his need for a rest. He ignored his Congressional responsibilities. He took control of the problem.

He explained in a *World* editorial. "Money must be raised to complete the pedestal for the Bartholdi statue. The *World* is the people's paper, and it now appeals to the people to come forward and raise this money." Almost immediately he received responses—two little boys sent one dollar, an office boy sent five cents, a "lonely and very aged woman" sent a dollar, an immigrant sent two dollars. A flood of small donations poured into the newspaper.

The project moved along so well that Pulitzer and his family left for Europe in May. His nerves were on edge. Massages and spa water did not help. He suffered from insomnia, and in his sleeplessness, he read the *World* and other papers sent to him daily. He demanded long reports from his management. He answered all these reports in detail. For all the work he did, he might as well have been in New York.

The pedestal project continued. By August 11, the *World* announced that it had collected $100,000 in donations, enough to build the pedestal. Once again, Pulitzer had engineered a spectacular crusade, a project that involved thousands of people, and, of course, brought new readers to the *World.*

Pulitzer bought a new invention, the quadruple press, which allowed him to produce pages faster and more easily than the old machine. With this purchase, Pulitzer had the best-equipped printshop in town.

He continued to print lots of pictures, far more than competing papers, although the process was expensive. First, an artist made a sketch. Then he transferred it into a pen and ink drawing with thick coarse lines. Then he sent the drawing to be photographed on zinc. Engravers etched in the spaces between the lines with acid. Then this cut was taken to the pressroom, put on blocks, and printed onto the paper. Each of these tasks had to be done with extreme care despite deadlines.

Pulitzer felt that he had a special responsibility because he printed so many sensational stories. This responsibility was to make sure that the stories were accurate down to the last detail. He would not let the sensationalism of the moment put him in jeopardy of a case of libel. He plastered the walls of his building with signs that said "Accuracy! Accuracy! Accuracy!" To back up this commitment, he sometimes fined a reporter who made a mistake. A reporter who over-estimated a crowd at 10,000 paid a fine because the actual number was closer to 5,000.

A few of his public service projects failed. He bought a field for his employees to use for sports, but it was too far from the shop. He tried to create a *World* village of home sites for his staff, but workers chose to be independent in their choice of living arrangements. He proposed a few plans for mutual financial investments, but the employees were not interested.

On the positive side, he paid better than average salaries. He paid a bonus for especially admirable work. He offered prizes for news ideas, editorials, and headlines. In return, he expected his workers to put the paper ahead of themselves and their families. He explained the way he saw the life of an editor of a large paper: "He must never go home to dinner without feeling sick, if the paper is beaten, if it is dull or poor."

In his head, he could devise super-human goals for himself. But his body could not keep up, and he continually suffered from the same complaints—insomnia, indigestion, and general nervousness. Paranoia became a part of his life. He worried that employee negligence might lead to lawsuits. He worried that workers were not following his orders. Workers learned to judge his moods. They knew that he was most approachable in the morning. As the afternoon wore on, he became more and more irritable. He did not spare Kate or the children. After one spat, Kate wrote in her diary: "[He said] I did not understand, had never been taught to understand the duties of a wife he then ordered me out of the room."

Fellow legislators questioned his increasingly frequent absences from Congress. They asked him how he could serve as a congressman if he did not attend meetings. He answered that he knew he could not serve both his paper and his constituency. In April 1886, he resigned from Congress.

He was happy to be back at the *World* full time. The paper was doing very well; circulation was now 170,000 daily and 230,000 on Sundays. With a strong sense of relief, Pulitzer paid off his debt to Gould. He bought a grand new house and furnished it with many art objects, including engravings and paintings.

But his pleasure at being back at the *World* full-time was short-lived. He was particularly sensitive to heat, and the spring and summer were very hot. Added to this physical problem was a social one. The Pulitzers had earned their right to be part of high society by virtue of the status of the paper and their personal fortune. But they were not welcome everywhere. Pulitzer had spoken widely and loudly against the accumulation of wealth, and the failure of the rich to care for the poor. His self-imposed duty to help the poor had lost him some friendships and perhaps some important connections. One of his editors said of him: "Mr. Pulitzer has no friends and no enemies. He has no policy that interferes with facts."

Added to the social problems were political ones that overwhelmed him. Pulitzer had invested time and money toward the campaign of Grover Cleveland, but the newly elected president's apparent favoritism of the rich disturbed him. He agonized over continuing fraud in the city government. He uncovered, but could not halt, corruption in the transportation system as the city changed from busses to streetcars.

He complained of asthma, weak lungs, stomach problems, insomnia, exhaustion, and depression. He experienced wide changes in mood from kindness to cruelty, from optimism to pessimism, and from wasteful spending to penny-pinching.

His family problems added to his suffering. His wife was pregnant again. Seven-year-old Ralph was not well. Six-year-old Lucille suffered from something that seemed like typhoid. Pulitzer could not take the strain. He sailed to Europe for a rest on June 20, 1886, the day after Edith Pulitzer was born. But he did not rest. In the month that he was gone, he sent many cables to both the W*orld* and the *Post-Dispatch*, constantly worrying about the businesses. When he got back, he worried about politics as well as business as he studied the candidates and issues for New York City's mayoral race and for the election of aldermen.

In the middle of the campaign, he worked on the ceremony for the unveiling of the Statue of Liberty. A military parade followed by thousands of spectators marched by the *World* building and down to the harbor. Pulitzer hired two steamships to take *World* employees to what was now Liberty Island for the best view of the dedication ceremonies. To keep the memory of his project alive, Pulitzer added a sketch of the statue to the masthead of the *World*.

According to an often-told story, Pulitzer could not control his temper at work. The story says that Joseph Howard, a reporter, frequently objected to his assignments. At one point, Pulitzer insisted that he cover a commonplace event. Howard insisted on covering a winter carnival in Montreal. They quarreled. As Howard aimed a blow at Pulitzer, he knocked his own glasses off. He asked Pulitzer

When Charles Dana started the *New York Evening Sun,* Pulitzer retaliated by putting out an afternoon version of the *New York World.*

to wait while he picked them up. Pulitzer did not wait. He picked up the reporter by his collar and the seat of his pants and threw him out of the room.

Until the late 1880s, there were few evening newspapers in New York, and none were important. Then in March 1887, publisher Charles Dana started a popular evening newspaper, the *Evening Sun*. This threatened to be competition for the *World*. Pulitzer responded immediately. He hired the *Sun*'s top writer away from that paper and onto his own staff. He put out an *Evening World*, a four-page one-penny newspaper. Before long, the paper outsold the *Evening Sun*.

Dana retaliated by calling Pulitzer the "Jew who does not want to be a Jew" and declared that Pulitzer was a traitor to his heritage. In retaliation, Pulitzer accused the *Sun* of borrowing $175,000 under false pretenses. Soon, articles and editorials in each paper appeared daily with insults for the competitor. The *Sun* always ended its articles with "Move On, Pulitzer, Move On."

A blood vessel ruptured in one of Pulitzer's eyes. The doctor told him that the eyesight in his other eye was deteriorating. If he wanted to save his vision, he would have to spend six weeks in a darkened room. This six-week period added to his mental exhaustion and frustration. The treatment may have saved him from going completely blind then, but from that time on he could not see well enough to read normal print. Pulitzer hired secretaries and aides to read to him and keep him up on the latest news and rumors.

In New York, there was a movement to change the state constitution. The change would make it harder for corrupt officials to trade jobs and contracts in return for votes and campaign donations. But state legislators refused to submit a ballot to the public, which would let citizens vote on whether to hold a constitutional convention to make the changes. Knowing that legislators were afraid of losing their political control, Pulitzer provided 5,000,000 ballots on the question. The proposition passed.

Pulitzer did not win all his fights in that November election. His chosen candidate for district attorney lost, a victim of the power of Tammany. Then he faced another defeat. Governor David Hill vetoed the measure to allow a constitutional convention. What Pulitzer had considered a victory for the *World* became worthless.

As always, his dejection led to ever more serious health problems. His nerves were shattered, and his eyesight dimmed. In the winter of 1888, his doctors advised him to go to the warmer climate of Monterey, California for the winter. Feeling unable to cope, Pulitzer took the advice. With a secretary/companion, he left St. Louis to find rest and relaxation.

He was on an impossible mission. This man had built his life on worry and work. He was unable to live without worry. Away from the responsibilities of the paper and city he loved, he became more nervous, more depressed, and more irritable.

Chapter Five

A Lonely Man

He returned to New York no better than when he left. Possibly because of his failing sight, he spent more and more time away from the office. He kept in very close contact through a multitude of memos that kept his secretaries busy reading and answering for him.

Still dissatisfied with doctors' diagnoses and prescriptions, Pulitzer decided to go to Europe to meet with specialists there. A British doctor confirmed the diagnosis of the American doctor and, like the American, advised his patient to stay away from any activities that would cause anxiety. Unhappy with this decision, Pulitzer consulted a doctor in Paris. He received the same warning. He was told that the arteries of his brain might harden and cause a stroke. His only safeguard was to stay calm.

For a short time he tried to entertain himself. He spent some time shopping, buying paintings, wine, and jewelry in Paris. He and Kate attended some social functions, including dinners with friends and a charity ball. In England he had an idea for creating a transatlantic newspaper with a central office in London. He was unable to negotiate a deal.

When he arrived back in America, he bought some Park Row property that gave him double pleasure. His first pleasure came in anticipation of a brand new office building, larger and more efficient than the old one. His second pleasure came from the fact that the building would be right across the street from the *Sun* and was much more handsome than Dana's building. He gloated in the paper: "Even the shabby little building of the *Sun* will be benefited by the splendor of its near neighbor."

He was back in Germany when he learned that the cornerstone of the new Pulitzer Building had been laid. His four-year-old son, Joseph, dressed in a blue and white sailor suit, hit the cornerstone with a silver trowel and said three times, "It is well done." Pulitzer sent a telegram beginning with "God grant that this structure be the enduring home of a newspaper forever unsatisfied with merely printing news—forever fighting every form of Wrong."

He simply could not stay away from America in the fall when election season heated up. He was determined to work in city, state, and national elections. His eyes were somewhat improved; his nerves were not. A staff member said that "whenever anything went wrong, and things seemed to go wrong with him very often, there would come from his office a stream of profanity and filth."

The winter of 1888 and 1889 was particularly difficult for Pulitzer, despite the birth of Constance in December. He suffered greatly from depression, insomnia, and general nervousness. The stresses of work and family weighed more heavily on him than before. During this time, his relationship with Kate suffered. With her increased family responsibilities, Kate could not accept the demands imposed by her husband's depression and his desire to control even the smallest details of his family's life.

The family hoped that another trip to Europe might help. He, Kate, Ralph, and Lucille journeyed together. He rushed from doctor to doctor hoping in vain to find one who would tell him that he could live just as he wanted to. Between doctor visits, he kept six secretaries busy reading to him and accepting the dictation of his many notes back to the *World*. Occasionally, he would ask a secretary to go horseback riding or for a walk with him. During these outings, Pulitzer usually talked about politics. He declared that he liked plays and operas, but he seldom sat through a whole performance. Because he could not see, he became bored quickly. He hired a "musical" secretary to play piano for him whenever he asked.

One doctor thought he discovered a way to keep Pulitzer from working. He told him to keep on the go, to keep traveling. The doctor was wrong. Pulitzer sent detailed schedules of his travels so that workers at the *World* could keep in almost constant touch with him. He gave detailed instructions for *World* employees in New York to forward mail to him wherever he was along the way. Once he said he wanted to hear only good news about the paper. Then he said he wanted to hear bad news so that he could help with the problems. Then he said that he wanted to hear everything, both positive and negative. He wrote detailed instructions about the building project, adding a great archway entrance and a gilded dome to the architect's plans. Occasionally he wrote to congratulate a writer on an article and to challenge him to keep doing excellent work.

Elizabeth Cochrane had proved herself a valuable investigative reporter for the *World*. Pulitzer hired her to create a sensational series of articles. Her task was to travel around the world faster than the character in *Around the World in Eighty Days,* a popular novel by Jules Verne. Using the pen name "Nellie Bly," she sent back regular reports to the *World* as she made her journey. All over the country, citizens followed the exploits of this most unusual woman. *World* circulation soared as readers waited breathlessly for each article. They cheered wildly when she finished her trip in just over seventy-two days. Pulitzer cheered too, partly for Cochrane and partly for the increased readership for the *World.*

An experience in Constantinople, Turkey renewed his worst fears. Arriving in the harbor, he mentioned that the day was exceptionally dark. His secretaries had to tell him that it was broad daylight. "It's

Elizabeth Cochrane assumed the alias "Nellie Bly" before taking a trip around the world in only seventy-two days.

dark to me," he answered, and he understood beyond a doubt that he had very little vision left. No one could take this news easily. How much harder it was for Pulitzer, whose nerves were fragile and whose career and life were built on reading and writing.

He hastened back to Europe, determined to consult with a specialist who could help him. In Naples, he lay in a darkened room, trying to build strength for a visit to a doctor. He could not do it. The room was near a military base, and frequent sounds of heavy artillery increased his problems. His secretaries decided that a move to St. Moritz, Switzerland might afford him the peace and quiet he needed. That plan didn't work either because the chilly mountain air gave him bronchitis.

Mrs. Pulitzer arrived from New York, hoping that she had brought the answer to his problems. That answer was Dr. George Hosmer, a physician. She hoped that the combination of Hosmer's medical advice and his attention as a friend would furnish the medicine that her husband needed. Hosmer described his patient in his diary: "[he] passed days on a sofa...it was a physical strain for him to cross the room and sit at the table." The doctor spent hours reading to his patient, describing the progress of the Pulitzer Building in detail, and discussing current events. Talk of politics may have been an important part of the "cure." By September, Pulitzer was eager to get back home and to immerse himself in his business, the new building, and the 1890 congressional elections.

That energy did not last long. In October, he announced in the paper: "Yielding to the advice of his physicians, Mr. Joseph Pulitzer has withdrawn entirely from the editorship of the *World*." He signed over the control of the *World* to an executive board of principal editors. He said readers would notice little or no change since this board had been substituting for him for several years. He made himself president of the Pulitzer Publishing Company.

It was almost immediately obvious that Pulitzer had no intention of withdrawing entirely from the paper to which he had given his life for six years. It is true that he did not go near the office. But it also is true that he met with a steady stream of executives at his home, conferring with each one in detail about the paper. He made just two concessions to his failing sight. He spent time and effort trying to study the faces of his wife and children, hoping to impress them in his memory. He also began negotiating for a yacht with the idea that this would help him to relax and perhaps even enjoy his forced retirement.

On December 10, 1890, the twelfth anniversary of Pulitzer's takeover of the *Dispatch*, the new *World* building was officially opened. The twenty stories of this tallest structure in New York rose over 300 feet, towering over City Hall. Pulitzer took some pleasure in the knowledge that his building was the first one seen by passengers entering the New York harbor from Europe. He was proud to announce, in bold headlines, that the two million dollar building was his without mortgage or debt.

One person was conspicuously missing from the gala celebration. That person was forty-three-year-old Pulitzer. He believed that the excitement would have overwhelmed him, so he left for Europe the day before the opening.

His secretary wrote to Kate from the ship that her husband's appetite was good and that he slept well. He added: "I can conscientiously say that you would be pleased, were you here, at the change for the better." On that same trip, Pulitzer wrote Kate: "I really feel that my health is broken and gone and that I cannot in reason expect to regain it...care and peace seem beyond my reach." Once an aide described him: "A man with a most astonishing range of conversation. Tall, cadaverous, reddish beard piercing but dead eyes, long bony hands; a fascinating yet terrible figure. He is not quite blind, but cannot see to read even with the most powerful glasses."

At first, he tried to control himself, to stay away from any talk of politics or business. Someone gave him some large-numeral playing cards, and he played games with his secretaries. He played chess with over-size pieces. He asked his secretaries to read fiction to entertain him. But he could not cure his insomnia. Before long, he complained to doctors that cutting him off from news of the *World* was cutting off his lifeblood. He demanded to hear news from New York. That news was both good and bad. The good news was that profits hit a record-breaking high. The bad news was that circulation was down.

He moved back into high gear. He sent instructions to fire one of his managing editors and to transfer another to the *Post-Dispatch*. Then he made arrangements to return to America as soon as possible. On June 3, he sailed for New York.

Once again, New York was the wrong place for a man with Pulitzer's sensitivity to heat. A particularly warm spell was oppressive even to the hardiest New Yorkers. He knew that he could not stay long in the city, so he bought a yacht for $100,000. He hired a naval officer to command the boat for him and anchored it in the North River, hoping to sail it to Europe as soon as he could leave the office. But one night on the ship convinced him otherwise. He simply could not stand the heat in the suffocating cabin.

Before making plans to sail to Europe on a commercial vessel, he spent another week in New York. He made some more changes in the management of the *World* and he announced the beginning of a series of five-year scholarships to City College of New York. Just one week after arriving in America, he sailed back to Europe on a commercial ship, his vision a little dimmer and suffering from insomnia and asthma.

In Germany, Pulitzer kept close contact with news from America. He held a weekly conference with aides to discuss potential stories for the *World*. He received regular copies of the W*orld*, the *Times,* the *Daily Telegraph,* the *Daily Mail,* the *Morning Post,* the *Daily News,* the *Westminster Gazette, Truth,* the *Spectator,* the *Saturday*

Pulitzer was proud of the new Pulitzer Building when it was opened in 1890, but he did not attend the official opening cermonies because the excitement would overwhelm him.

Review, the *Nation,* the *Outlook,* and other publications that his staff believed might interest him. His secretaries skimmed the papers, choosing those articles they thought most likely to please him. After listening to items read to him, Pulitzer directed the assignment of stories. Among the topics were the persecution of Jews in Russia, the need for a public playground in the East River project, and the *World*'s claim that James Blaine, once again favored by some as a presidential candidate, was unfit for the office.

He was accomplishing a great deal, but Pulitzer's health continued to decline. He became increasingly sensitive to noise. His friends and aides tried to protect him from loud voices, traffic sounds, and even the normal sounds that accompany everyday living. But they were not always successful. Pulitzer reacted to these failures with one of two moods—rage or depression. Whatever his reaction, it was always accompanied by more persistent insomnia. Worse still, he suspected even his most faithful aides, accusing them of deliberately harassing him and of doing things behind his back. He made this situation worse by trying to enlist some of his aides as spies to report on the others. He told an acquaintance, "I am the loneliest man in the world," complaining that some people were afraid to befriend him for fear that he would find out something about them that he would reveal in the paper.

Finally, he believed that he should prepare himself to die. So he sailed to New York in October to prepare his will.

He wanted to leave a legacy to publishing. He entered into negotiations with Columbia University to establish a school of journalism. These negotiations failed. He could not find a trustee who believed that journalism was a profession of enough value to have a school devoted to teaching it.

Chapter Six

A Strong Competitor

That summer Joseph Pulitzer became interested in the plight of strikers in Homestead, Pennsylvania. These steel workers protested against low wages and unsafe working conditions. Pulitzer strongly supported the *World* editorial that defended the strikers. But he changed his mind when he found out that the strikers had seized the plant. He said that this seizure was illegal, and he could not support anyone who broke the law. Pulitzer was widely criticized for changing his mind.

During another strike, this one of railway workers, the *World's* editorial pages supported government intervention. Because of its anti-striker stand, the *World* lost some readers and some advertisers.

Pulitzer traveled to spas at Wiesbaden and Baden-Baden in Germany, hoping for rest and relaxation. Insomnia and depression still attacked him, but not enough to stop him from working. From Germany, he wrote continually to his editors, scolding them for not working hard enough and for not checking accuracy of articles.

In particular, he nagged at George Harvey, the managing editor. After many notes and letters of negative criticism, Pulitzer wrote to him: "As long as I find fault with you, I hope and believe in the use of trying to train, teach, and perpetuate you. When I find it hopeless to improve a man, I always quit the job and never criticize." As proof that he was not merely criticizing, he told Harvey how to improve himself and his performance. For a first step, he should spend six hours a day reading papers. Then he should spend two to three hours a day reading books. Then, and only then, could be become a managing editor good enough for the *World*.

Harvey was not his only frustration. He spent sleepless nights and irritable days thinking about politicians whom he believed to be dishonest. When he learned that a superintendent of prisons flogged the inmates, Pulitzer demanded his removal. He kept up his crusade until the superintendent, whom he dubbed "The Paddler," was removed from his job.

With another part of his mind he worried about how to celebrate the tenth anniversary of his purchase of the *World*. He had to make his plans for the anniversary while he was on the ship. He could not put up with the emotional strain of working in the New York office. He gave orders that the one hundred page anniversary edition would come out on the night he docked. As he stepped from the ship, aides were to hand him this special edition, more than twice as big as a normal paper. That night he planned a dinner for selected members of his staff at the elegant Delmonico's restaurant.

Always on the lookout for a secretary who could read well, converse intelligently, and yield to his wishes, Pulitzer kept looking for the perfect companion. He hired a staff member with the sole job of helping him to travel and to find quarters that would not offend his increasing sensitivity to noise and confusion.

As his vision dimmed, his hearing became more acute. Secretaries and aides read to him incessantly—plays, novels, biographies, and, of course, newspapers. He often went to the theater. There his biggest problem was his acute hearing that seemed to magnify every cough and rustle from the audience. He often compared plays unfavorably to newspaper stories. He complained that playwrights should write in the same snappy and concise style as journalists.

In October 1893, he sailed for Paris. He had hardly stepped off the ship before he declared that Paris noise was overwhelming. He fled to Nice where his aide had found an apartment on the coast that could be soundproofed and where Pulitzer would not be assaulted by noisy plumbing, barking from neighbors' dogs, or other such noises.

Back at home, Ralph suffered with both a heart condition and pneumonia. Ralph and Kate decided that the climate and living style in St. Moritz, Switzerland, might help him to recuperate. Pulitzer joined them briefly but found that the strain of family relationships took time from his newspaper duties and irritated him. He left for Austria where he could feel free from family problems.

Back in the United States, an economic depression dampened the spirits of Americans. Millions were unemployed, banks failed, and government finances were weak. The union for the Pullman Railroad called a strike, which threatened to paralyze personal and commercial transportation, and the mail. Pulitzer came back to America to play some part in the fall elections. With the support of the *World*, the Republican candidate won the race for mayor of New York City. Democrats lost badly in many races.

That same year, his brother Albert sold the *New York Morning Journal* to the publisher of the *Cincinnati Enquirer* for $1,000,000. The paper lost money, and the new owner sold it the next year to William Randolph Hearst, publisher of the *San Francisco Examiner*. Here was strong competition for the *World*. William Hearst invested generously to improve the *Journal*. He increased the number of pages in the paper, and he lowered the price from two cents to a penny. Hearst's newspaper was much like Pulitzer's. Both appealed to the working class, used simple language, and wrote about entertainment, crusades, and sensationalism. Both papers also supported public protest against corruption.

Although he was seldom home, Pulitzer wanted his household to run as though he were there all the time. Angry with Kate, he once wrote: "don't you think you should have written me, no matter how angry you felt. Don't you think you should have written about the children at least? Am I not entitled to that much?" He tried in vain to find his kind of peace at Chatwold, Maine. He built a soundproofed four-story granite tower-like structure there. In the basement, he built a steam-heated swimming pool. In this building, he was safe from noise—except for the occasional foghorn. Pulitzer entertained lavishly at Chatwold. He fed an average of over fifty people every day, counting guests, servants, secretaries, and other staff.

Living with his wife and children was impossible for him. By the late 1890s, Kate saw her husband only a few weeks of each year for brief periods of time. When his son Joseph entered St. Mark's Preparatory School, Pulitzer sent instructions to the headmaster. He wanted his son to be taught history, geography, the English language, and a thorough knowledge of America. He also demanded that Joseph develop good reading habits and a strong memory. He sent him a copy of Plutarch's *Lives* by a first century Greek biographer. He told his young son to choose a hero from that book and to follow his example.

When his sixth child Herbert was born in November 1895, Pulitzer could see him only dimly. In an attempt to perceive as much as he could, he hired an artist to make pictures of his whole family. The artist made black thick-lined drawings on white paper for Pulitzer.

In December 1895, President Grover Cleveland's actions goaded Pulitzer back into the political arena. The president intervened in a dispute between England and Venezuela over territorial rights. He based this intervention on the 1823 Monroe Doctrine, which said that the United States would oppose all European intervention in independent countries in the Americas. Cleveland threatened to send in American troops if England did not settle the matter peacefully.

Pulitzer felt a surge of energy when he heard of Cleveland's threat. He whipped off an editorial against the President, saying that the Monroe Doctrine did not apply here: "To interfere in South America and bring on a war between two great, free and highly civilized

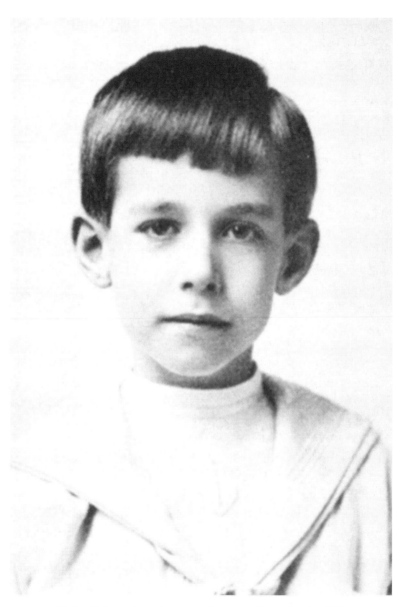

Herbert Pulitzer, shown here at age five, was Pulitzer's favorite child.

nations on any account less serious than a menace would be the monumental crime of the century." He added a warning about the contagion of war: "Let the war once dominate the minds of the American people and war will come whether there is cause for it or not." Taking an unpopular view, Pulitzer declared that the United States should keep hands off: "It [the dispute] is not our frontier. It is none of our business "

He pushed further. He sent hundreds of cables to British leaders, urging them to send messages of peace back to America so that Pulitzer could publish them in the *World*. Many of these messages appeared on the front page of the *World* on Christmas morning.

The American secretary of state announced that Pulitzer might be guilty of treason. He said that a 1799 statute prohibited citizens from carrying on correspondence with a foreign government with intent to influence them. He threatened Pulitzer with a fine of $5,000 and imprisonment up to three years. New York Police Commissioner Theodore Roosevelt declared that he would be glad to impose the punishment.

In the pages of the *World*, Pulitzer happily pleaded guilty and dared officials to impose the punishment. The talk died down. Negotiations averted a war without a battle, and the *World* announced that its "publicity had done its work."

Pulitzer planned another trip abroad to rest. He sailed to London and went on to the Kensington Gardens. The shrieking of the royal peacocks in the park upset him. In vain, his aides tried to get them silenced. Pulitzer left to search for other places in England where he could be comfortable.

His paranoia grew. Fearful that a competitor would intercept cables going across the Atlantic, he devised a code with special names for important staff members, the president, and other government leaders, and for financial terms such as circulation and advertising revenue. When he sent a cable to New York about advertising revenue

William Randolph Hearst bought the *New York Morning Journal* and became Pulitzer's biggest competitor for working class readers.

loss, he referred to advertising as "Potash Pigeon." He signed his cables "Andes." The governor was called "Mediocrity," the president, "Graving," and the Democratic Party, "Gosling." He created a thick codebook for these special words, and he gave copies of the book to his top management.

One day in early 1896, Hearst hired away his whole Sunday edition staff, including the editor. The very next day, Pulitzer hired them back by offering them more money. One day later, Hearst countered with even more money, and the staff went back to him. Pulitzer gave up. He immediately assembled the best staff he could find on the spur of the moment, and he was able to put out a Sunday edition.

After he had a few days to consider what Hearst had done to him, he devised a plan to get even. He dropped the price of the *World* to a penny. He believed that this would bring in new readers, probably many of them from the *Journal*. At the same time, he would increase his profit margin by raising advertising rates, telling his advertisers that he expected many new readers.

His plan didn't work. Although he dropped the price of the paper, he gained few new subscribers. Advertisers refused to pay higher rates, especially since Pulitzer failed to get the expected increase in circulation. Some advertisers dropped their ads entirely. They said they would advertise again only when Pulitzer lowered the rates.

Pulitzer now saw only one option, and that was to cut costs. He reduced the number of pages in the paper. Hearst opened a campaign of posters and billboards to advertise his *Journal*. Many readers, both of the *World* and the *Journal*, enjoyed anticipating the next move in the competition. They dubbed the newspapers "The Yellow Press" because both papers featured a cartoon called "Yellow Kids" in which the main character wore a bright yellow dress.

The competition for newspaper employees continued. Pulitzer scheduled a dinner to honor an especially effective employee. The day before the dinner, that employee joined Hearst's staff. Pulitzer cancelled the dinner. A short time later, a Pulitzer employee resigned in anger against his employer and in a few days, he was happily working for Hearst. The publisher of the *Journal* promised potential employees something that Pulitzer did not. He promised that especially good writers would get their own by-line—their name printed above a newspaper article—telling who wrote it.

Journal circulation rose to 150,000. This was uncomfortably close to the circulation of the *World*. Four smaller papers suffered— the *Advertiser,* the *Mercury*, the *Press*, and the *Recorder*. This brought the *Journal* and the *World* neck and neck in the race for readers. As a formidable opponent, Hearst received his own code name. He was known as "Gush."

Pulitzer had a big advantage over Hearst in ready money. Pulitzer had a personal fortune of about $8 million, an annual profit from his newspapers of almost half a million dollars, and a huge portfolio of investments. Hearst received only $100,000 a year from his profitable San Francisco *Examiner*. The rest of his money came from his widowed mother. Speculation flew—when would Mrs. Hearst decide to cut off these gifts to her son?

Another difference in the two operations was that Hearst spent little on news gathering. Rather, he picked up his news from other papers, notably from the *World*. It was rumored that when an edition of the *World* arrived in the *Journal* offices, teasers would chant: "sound the cymbals, beat the drum/ The *World* is here, the news has come."

Pulitzer caught the election bug again in 1896 when Republican William McKinley ran against Democrat William Jennings Bryan for president. Pulitzer did not want a Republican in the presidency, but neither did he support Bryan's financial programs. For this race, Pulitzer thought it best to focus on the issues rather than on a single candidate. He wrote telegrams, letters, and editorials supporting

McKinley's programs. This grueling work appeared to revive him; Pulitzer seemed healthier than he had in a long time. McKinley won by almost 600,000 popular votes.

Now Pulitzer really needed a vacation. He sailed for the Mediterranean. His ship docked in Monte Carlo, but the sounds of the other boats in the harbor and of the hotels and resorts on the coast overwhelmed him. His staff moved him to a hotel on a more isolated peninsula, but even there they could not control the day-to-day living noises that bothered Pulitzer. He wrote to Kate that he loved her and was eager to see her. He added that he had not written because he could think of nothing to say except to complain. He also told her to tell the children that he did not love them because they did not write to him.

For two months, he consulted with many doctors. He accepted some of their advice about diet, massage, and baths. He refused to accept advice to stop working and otherwise avoid stress. He returned to America feeling no better than when he had left.

Pulitzer thought that he had kept in close touch with his staff while he was away. He almost collapsed when he discovered that he had not been informed about recent changes in the Sunday paper. The editors had doubled the comics from four to eight pages. They had increased the number of sensational articles. The changes were so drastic that some Sunday school teachers were protesting against the paper. Some clubs cancelled their subscriptions. *World* editors told Pulitzer that they made the changes to keep up readership in the face of still strong competition from the *Journal*. Pulitzer would not accept this answer. He insisted that his staff could retain the integrity of the press no matter what Hearst did.

Immediately, he put tight curbs on spending. He checked the bills that came into the *World*, and he accused some creditors of padding their costs. He cut Kate's allowance, and he complained about everything new that he saw in the house. Then, as though he had never

Although he usually supported Democrats, Pulitzer wrote editorials to defeat William Jennings Bryan, the Democratic candidate for president in 1896.

started this attack on extravagance, he tried to buy a luxury mansion in the city. This deal fell through. But he did add to the scholarship fund he had set up at Teachers' College. And he sent money to relatives in Hungary.

Chapter Seven

A Welcome to War

In 1897, seventeen-year-old Lucille Irma Pulitzer celebrated her coming-out with an elegant party in September. Lucille was brilliant, charming, and hard working; a very promising young lady. A couple of weeks after her party, she came down with typhoid. On December 31, she died. After the funeral, Pulitzer left for a vacation. A month later, he resumed his detailed criticisms of the paper.

Reports from Cuba were full of the torture, jailing, and slaughter of Cuban rebels by Spanish rulers. Pulitzer sided with the colonials in their rebellion against the Spanish. The *World* and the *Journal* became even fiercer competitors. Each paper sent reporters to Cuba with instructions to capture the drama of the situation and to attract more readers than the other paper. News flowed from the little island, articles full of words like bloody, hideous, defenseless, butchery, and massacre. Photos of rebels in crowded and unsanitary concentration camps accompanied these articles. A typical *World* headline blared: "Blood on the roadsides, blood in the fields, blood on the doorsteps, blood, blood, blood!" Although Pulitzer usually insisted on his rule of Accuracy! Accuracy! Accuracy!, he did not criticize the reports from Cuba, even when he knew they were exaggerated. He approved of the way his managing editor invented and used new type for headlines. These large block letters screamed from the front pages.

Articles in both papers encouraged American readers to take a stand against the Spanish. They encouraged them to support strong action against Spain, expressed impatience with President McKinley and his talk of peaceful negotiation, and shouted their outrage at the atrocities. They bombarded the public with stories of Spaniards raping Cuban women, butchering wounded prisoners, torturing and robbing. The papers agreed about the war; they disagreed only on the question of which paper had the most readers.

To attract more readers and advertisers, Hearst copied some of Pulitzer's most successful public relations gimmicks. He opened a soup kitchen, hired bands and held firework displays, and sponsored benefit performances at the Opera House. Of course, these philanthropies and celebrations got major headlines in the *Journal,* and they attracted more readers.

Pulitzer reacted with more belt-tightening. He sent out messages to his staff: "I want a radical reduction of expenses from beginning to end of every department." Then he went a step further. He asked for "spies" to infiltrate the *Journal,* to learn about their short- and long-term plans, hoping to thwart them.

Pulitzer was able to accomplish all this without stepping foot in the offices of the *World.* Because of his wide network of information gatherers, he could operate well from Jekyll Island, Georgia, from Bar Harbor, Maine, or from Europe. Besides having newspapers read to him daily, he maintained dozens of other sources of information through friends, reports, contacts, magazines, and letters. Because of his almost encyclopedic memory, he was aware whenever a reporter violated the truth. He kept extremely close tabs on office workers. He asked his top managers for reports on employees, detailing the exact hours each man worked and including a summary of his character and temperament. Frequently, he sent a report to the man in question, and told him how he had collected the information.

As his health declined, he felt compelled to think about the

Lucille Irma Pulitzer died in 1897 at age seventeen.

previously unthinkable. Who would take over when he was no longer able to manage the *World*? He thought of a few men who had the qualifications—success in business, money, and newspaper experience. But each potential candidate fell short in one aspect or another.

His older sons seemed unlikely prospects to succeed him. Neither Ralph at Harvard nor Joseph at a prep school was doing well. Pulitzer furnished tutors. He expected both sons to do exceptionally well at school. He insisted that all his children write to him frequently, reporting class incidents, social lives, and even outlines of conversations. He complained that his sons were not respectful toward him, especially Ralph. Kate tried to help her sons to accept this kind of criticism. She told them that his attitude was a result of his nervous condition, not a symbol of his true feelings. She also explained to them that his temper and irritability increased during those times when he paid no attention to his diet and suffered from indigestion. He could not control himself--this man who controlled one of the most important newspapers in America and who was responsible for reform in city, state, and nation.

His goals for his daughters were different from those for his sons. He wanted them to be good mothers, efficient home managers, pleasant companions for their husbands, and responsible citizens. His daughters had private tutors to insure that they had intellectual interests. To further this, he told Kate to make sure that they read a lot. First, he said that they could read any books they wanted. But then he found out that Edith was reading some French novels.He admitted that he had said they could read anything, but "that naturally meant that the books must be proper and fit, subject to the mother's or governess' approval."

The conflict in Cuba deepened. A new Spanish government promised the Cuban rebels more freedom. But the rebels, perhaps encouraged by the *World* and the *Journal,* demanded full independence. The American battleship *Maine* traveled to Havana, to all intents and purposes for a friendly visit. But on the night of Feb. 15, 1898, the *Maine* exploded as it lay at anchor outside Havana. Two hundred-fifty American sailors were killed. The Spanish insisted that the blast had occurred from some crisis within the boat. The *World* suggested that Spanish treachery might be to blame. The *Journal*, with no more information than the *World*, lay the blame directly on Spain. Both papers urged immediate war with Spain.

Other newspapers criticized the *World* and the *Journal* for accusing the Spanish without verified information. American citizens tended to side with the "yellow journals," blaming the Spanish for the attack. The United States Senate passed a resolution to declare war against Spain by a vote of forty-two to thirty-five. The House passed the same resolution by a vote of 310 to six.

On May 7, E. W. Harden, reporter for the *World*, sent back the announcement: "The entire Spanish fleet of eleven vessels was destroyed. Three hundred Spaniards were killed and four hundred wounded. Our loss was none killed and but six slightly wounded." The *World* scored a scoop with this news, and the other American papers rushed to pick up the facts for their articles. In August, the defeated Spanish signed a truce with the United States.

In December, American and Spanish officials signed a peace treaty. The United States paid Spain $20,000,000 and acquired former Spanish territory in Cuba, Puerto Rico, the Philippines, and Guam, an island in the Pacific Ocean.

All in all, the *World* did not benefit from the war as much as Pulitzer had expected. He had hired special reporters, paid their transportation bills, and put out many extra editions. These extra expenses did not lead to the increased readership he needed to compete with Hearst. Except for Harden's story, the reporting did not attract much attention. Even Stephen Crane, author of *The Red Badge of Courage*, did not fulfill expectations as a reporter for the *World*.

Pulitzer had an idea to increase readership. He created a question-

and-answer section, which he called the "School House." Typical questions were fairly simple for an educated readership. All of them pertained to news of the day like "What are the Philippines?" and "What is a Malay?" and "What are some habits of the Malaysian people?" He published the questions in one edition, and the answers in another. This proved to be popular. His next idea was to win readers by cutting down on political articles in the paper. He asked his editors to try to go a month without injecting politics into the editorial page. He said that if anyone felt a strong need to write about politics, he should do so with humor. After a month, Pulitzer assessed the results of this de-emphasis on politics, and decided that it did not work. So he changed his mind about political writing. He told his editors that the editorial page had withered away to nothing, and he demanded strong opinions on the news of the day.

An early morning fire on January 9, 1900, forced Kate, Edith, Constance, and Herbert to flee from their 55th Street home, barefoot and in their nightclothes. Two servants were killed. Scores of paintings, tapestries, jewelry, and books were destroyed. Pulitzer stayed in his Lakewood, New Jersey home. From there, he sent sympathy to the family and staff. He also asked that a close friend come to cheer him up because of the bad news.

Despite his intense concern about personal and business economies, he hired an architect to draw up plans for a new $250,000 house. He asked the architect to draw the plans on the whitest paper with the blackest marker possible. He planned a five-story structure of limestone and granite. It included a library, a ballroom, and a swimming pool. He ordered that a plaster model be sent to him at Bar Harbor so that he could study it by touch.

He became the focus of a newspaper article when he bought the first motor-driven delivery truck to be used for newspaper delivery. He had plans for buying twenty more and for retiring the seventy horses then used for deliveries.

He asked his staff, relatives, and friends to help him look for another secretary. But he insisted that the final choice be left up to him because, he said, choosing a secretary was something like choosing a spouse. Among the requirements were that the man would eat quietly, breathe softly, use perfect manners, and never lose interest as a conversationalist. He was just as fussy with his own staff. He asked a member of his staff to tell editor Don Seitz that the noise of his chewing, particularly of food like toast, disturbed Pulitzer when they ate together. He enjoyed riding and always rode with a groom on one side and a secretary on the other. The secretary's job was to keep up a continuous conversation to interest Pulitzer, no matter what the speed of the horses or flatness of the terrain.

In April 1900, Pulitzer sailed for Liverpool with several servants, some secretaries, a couple of guests, and some riding horses. His aides spread a thick rope "carpet" on the deck above his elegant stateroom so the noise of footsteps above would not disturb him.

That same year, twenty-one-year-old Ralph graduated from Harvard. Pulitzer asked his managing editor to accept him as a clerk. He expected Ralph to work his way up through the ranks. Pulitzer told the editor to be strict with Ralph and to send frequent and detailed reports on his son's activities at the paper.

Before Pulitzer would move in to his new home, he assigned two men to stay in his bedroom for a night. Their task was to listen to see if the sounds of the New Haven or New York Central trains or the Madison Avenue trolley reached into the bedroom. They found no problem. Then one man stood outside the suite shouting at the top of his lungs, and he pounded on the floors. The man listening in Pulitzer's room declared the suite soundproof.

Just as Pulitzer tried to exert complete control over his environment, he tried to exert control over everyone near him. In many aspects of his life he was successful because of his domineering personality and his intellectual power. When he couldn't get what he wanted by demanding and badgering, he used self-pity. He told people that they had no idea how he suffered. He described in detail his insomnia, headaches, asthma, rheumatism, indigestion, diabetes, respiratory infections, and other ills.

He repeatedly told his children how lucky they were, especially in contrast to him. Once he wrote to Ralph: "I ask was there ever a human being in this world so truly forsaken and deserted and shamefully treated by fate, destiny, or family." Ralph spoke frankly to him. He summarized the financial assets of the paper and the number of awards and prizes won by the *World* staff. He said that a sick man could not have accomplished all that. He reminded his father that he had both family and staff to wait on him hand and foot. Pulitzer became angry and accused his son of ingratitude and lack of concern.

Kate learned to live with his moods, partly by ignoring him. He scolded her for spending too much money on dresses, and he said he would no longer pay those bills. He complained of her ingratitude: "the least you could have done would have been to give me a few words of appreciation." She frequently overspent her allowance. If her husband cut the amount of money he gave her, she simply spent what she wanted, and sent the bills to him. One month, after he had boosted her monthly allowance to $8,000, she spent $23,000. Forced to spend most of her time on her own, she flitted from New York to Europe to Florida. Once when writing to him for money, she said: "You should consider yourself very fortunate that you have such an economical wife, in fact my own feeling is that you should be a little ashamed of my parsimony."

Pulitzer told Kate never to cable him after lunch. He said that receiving cables in the afternoon excited him so much that he could not sleep at night. He went on to complain that neither his wife nor his children wrote to him often enough. No matter how long their letters were nor how often they wrote, Pulitzer complained. One frequent complaint was that the letters did not describe people fully enough. He wanted to know details of his children's acquaintances—the sounds of their voices, style of their clothes, and even their body measurements.

Sometimes he sought control by showering his children with gifts—a yacht and an automobile for the boys, jewels for the girls. He granted generous allowances, and sometimes added even more money than he had promised.

As for his professional life, Pulitzer could certainly count that a success. At fifty-three, he had been in the newspaper business for thirty-three years. He was probably the best-informed man in the country. His record of supporting liberalism and reform was admired by many. His few failures were probably due to his inability to control either his nerves or his ambitions.

Chapter Eight

No Peace or Quiet

In 1901, Pulitzer felt a strong need to get into the political arena again. The country had erupted in outrage when President Theodore Roosevelt invited black educator Booker T. Washington to lunch at the White House. Some citizens proclaimed that this invitation would lead to the downfall of white people in America. Pulitzer sprang to Roosevelt's support, chastising his critics.

Pulitzer tried again to get Columbia University to accept money to open a school of journalism. The trustees repeated that journalism was not a profession and therefore not worthy of a special school. Pulitzer persisted until they accepted his offer. But when he tried to gain control by naming the advisory board, they argued that neither Pulitzer nor the *World* should have authority over the creation of the school. Finally, Pulitzer gave in. He deposited the first million dollars with Columbia and sat back to see what they would do with it.

Early in 1904, the Pulitzer family moved into the 73rd Street mansion. Immediately, Pulitzer declared that his staffers had not done their job well. He found noise, and a lot of it, in the house. For one thing, a sump pump was working in the cellar. The heating system carried the noise of that pump directly to his room. He ordered that the walls be packed with mineral wool to deaden the sound. He was unable to stifle the noise of the elevator door in the hall outside his rooms, nor could he stop the noise made by the shrinking woodwork as it settled.

Pulitzer said the house was a failure. He was impatient with the solutions offered by the builders. He had a structure built just for himself, three doors away from the main house. In this double-walled building, parts of the floor rested on ball bearings to prevent vibration. Even in this annex, sometimes called the Vault, Pulitzer complained of trolley bells and whistles. Builders discovered that these street noises came through the fireplace chimney. They inserted frames holding thousands of silk threads to absorb vibrations. The outside sounds disappeared.

He admitted that the responsibility for the editorial page was more than he could bear at that time. Still, he continued to criticize it. Pulitzer wrote to Frank Cobb, a new editor: "You must try to write as little as possible, just as I did, but you must try to think just as I did, to suggest as hard as I did, to edit copy as I used to do and yet keep judgment, decision and responsibility in your own hands." Writing from a ship on the Baltic, he sent these reactions to articles by Cobb: " they present a very good example of what I detest." He added that he wanted Cobb to help Ralph.

During the spring and early summer of 1904, Pulitzer spent a lot of time at Bar Harbor, working on the presidential campaign. He might have stayed away from a campaign of less personal interest to him, but Hearst was running for the Democratic nomination. Pulitzer was relieved when Democrat Alton Parker received the nomination at the July convention. Pulitzer's relief did not last long. He was convinced that Parker was not trying hard enough, that he could never beat incumbent Republican Roosevelt. In *World* editorials, he tried and tried to encourage Parker to be bolder and more aggressive. He asked Parker to point out the fact that Roosevelt was two-faced, pandering to the ideas that would bring him votes. Parker refused to engage in these accusations. He lost to Roosevelt.

Even more important to Pulitzer than the election was the *World*. Pulitzer felt as though he had been struck when Cobb said he was going to resign. Pulitzer told him that he could not resign. After much conversation and argument, Pulitzer convinced him to stay with the *World*. They agreed not to be angry with each other at the same time. In a letter to Cobb, Pulitzer wrote: "you could not possibly please me more than by swearing to accept my criticism in the future without feeling hurt, even if it should seem to you very wrong."

In 1905, the *World* attacked corrupt insurance companies that had invested money and bought stocks without the consent of policyholders. In many cases, these financial moves made the insurance managers rich and drained the assets of the company. Reports in the *World* forced the governor to appoint a committee to investigate. Even Pulitzer was surprised at the extent of the corruption.

Whether on the seas or in Bar Harbor, Pulitzer kept up a steady stream of notes to the *World* offices. He kept close tabs on members of his staff. He cabled questions about particular articles, always seeking to know more than was written—questions about the motives of a person who was interviewed, suggestions for reform of the matter in focus, queries about the accuracy of the article.

He also cabled criticism of the paper, especially of the editorial page. He dictated that no editorials should be written about topics he considered unappealing to most readers—socialism, railroad rates, taxes and tariffs, to name a few. He complained that the editorial page was frequently "too dry, too melancholy, too much corruption."

Pulitzer objected when Ralph announced that he would marry Frederica Webb, granddaughter of William Henry Vanderbilt. Pulitzer doubted that the Webb or the Vanderbilt families were equipped with sufficient character and ideals to keep Ralph spurred on to ambition. He cross-examined Frederica at several different occasions.

Pulitzer's nerves strained almost to the breaking point. Frustrations piled up until he thought he could not handle another thing. He was unhappy about Ralph's choice of a bride. He was upset about Kate's extravagance. He was heartsick about Joseph who was warned

Shortly after moving into his new mansion on the Upper West side, Pulitzer said the house was a failure.

that he might be expelled for poor grades at Harvard. Not long after this warning, Joseph and some classmates sneaked out of the dormitory to buy beer. Since the dorm door was locked when they came back, they decided to climb in an open window. Joseph went first. That open window happened to be the bedroom window of the headmaster. Joseph was expelled.

To add to his distress, Pulitzer was jealous of artist John Singer Sargent, who had painted a very flattering portrait of Kate. And he was in despair about the weakness of the Democratic Party.

These frustrations, plus the strain of the wedding preparations and the ceremony, left him with a severe attack of diabetes. Right after the wedding, Pulitzer sailed for Europe, hoping to rest and recover during the trip.

When Ralph and Frederica returned from their honeymoon, they discovered still another wedding gift from Pulitzer. He had bought them a house next door to his on 73rd Street. Now Pulitzer could keep a close eye on his son.

Joseph, too, was always under his father's direction. Pulitzer asked his son to write a description of himself. Joseph wrote: "I think I have, so far, led a pretty useless sort of existence. My purpose in the past has always been to enjoy life...you have told me that I am no good and that the best thing I could do would be to get out, leave home, and shift for myself."

After his expulsion from Harvard, it was Joseph's turn to see how he would work out in the newspaper business. He worked at the *World* as a reporter. In his first two weeks on the job, he was late once and failed to come in to work two days. He was fired. His father sent him to the *Post-Dispatch* with detailed instructions, both for Joseph and for his supervisors. Those who worked near him were to make sure that he learned to be accurate and neat and also to be polite to everybody, including the office boy. The instructions continued: he was to learn advertising, circulation, and business practices. After just

After his expulsion from Harvard, Joseph Pulitzer Jr. (right) went to work at the *New York World*, but his father soon fired him for tardiness and missing work.

two weeks, he was to study all the machines in the building so that he thoroughly understood each one. He was to keep a daily diary in shorthand and to send his father reports at least twice a week. He was to meet the people introduced to him by his father's letters and to socialize with them. Pulitzer demanded frequent reports from every staff member at the paper who had any connection with Joseph.

In 1906, Pulitzer ordered a steam yacht designed for cruising and including a dining room, music room, sitting room, gymnasium, personal quarters for his attendants, and staterooms for guests. A crew of forty-five men ran the ship. "I love this boat," Pulitzer said, "In a house I am lost in my blindness, always fearful of falling on stairs or obstacles. Here, the narrow companionways give me safe guidance. Nothing in all my life has given me so much pleasure."

When Hearst ran for governor on the Independence League ticket, Pulitzer actually welcomed the entrance of his old foe into the race. He felt that the Democratic Party was so ineffective that almost any candidate would be better than a Democratic one. For a while, the race was too close to call, but in the end, Republican Charles Evans Hughes won by almost 60,000 votes.

Although he was glad that Hearst did not win, his concerns about the election so upset Pulitzer that he sailed for Europe again. This time he took eleven-year-old Herbert with him. He believed that Herbert was the brightest of all his children, and, though he said it was a sacrifice to him, he committed himself to making the most of Herbert's life.

In Greece, Pulitzer suffered both physically and mentally. When Kate offered to join him, he refused, saying that he was too sick. Then he complained that his family had abandoned him. Kate wrote to him: "you would be so much happier, my dear Joseph, if you would only believe the friendly intentions & good feeling of the people about you." He answered: "I want some love and affection from my children in the closing short span of life that still remains. If I cannot have that love and affection, I may expect to be spared the willful deliberate disrespect, disobedience and insult."

In April 1907, Pulitzer announced that he would celebrate his sixtieth birthday in both New York and St. Louis, with a party for sixty guests in each city. Invited guests were members of the staffs at the *World* and the *Post-Dispatch*. He planned the parties down to the last detail. But he didn't attend either one. He sent greetings to each party from Europe. At this time he sent to each paper an announcement that he would retire on his sixtieth birthday.

The *Post-Dispatch* followed his orders to print the retirement announcement. But Cobb of the *World* suspected that the announcement was simply an attempt to get attention. The *World* did not print the announcement.

Pulitzer named Ralph acting head of the *World* and president of the *Post-Dispatch*. He did not mention Joseph. Apparently, he felt that Joseph was not yet ready for a title and the responsibilities behind it.

As Pulitzer's close staff and friends suspected, he did not remove his influence from either paper. However, he did admit to Cobb that he was unsure of himself. He wrote: "I might send you an order that would mean a change in the paper's policy. I want you to make me a promise. If I ever do such a thing, swear that you will ignore my wishes."

Then he fell into emotional turmoil again after he commissioned a bust of himself by the famous sculptor Auguste Rodin. The problem was that he hated the idea of showing any of his body. Rodin wanted him to bare his shoulders so that he could get a full picture of Pulitzer's neck. When Pulitzer refused, Rodin said he would give up the commission. Finally, Pulitzer agreed. But he was so angry at being defeated that he refused to talk during the posing. This made it difficult for Rodin, who wanted to display his subject in a natural pose.

Despite his "retirement," Pulitzer continued his crusades. He continued to fight against the tradition that forbade entertainment on Sunday. He ordered his staff to create a Sunday section focusing on the beauty of music and the other arts. He told them to discuss historical eras of censorship and to show how the lack of arts robbed the people of an important potential aspect of their lives.

Despite his blindness, he was determined to appreciate the arts, especially writing. The records show that he had read about a hundred books a year for twenty-one years. He also read thousands of newspapers, magazines, letters, and reports.

He kept close tabs on his employees, particularly those in higher management. When he heard that some of his editors were harassing Managing Editor George Harvey, he wired from Bar Harbor: "Tell Cobb, Seymour, etc. to treat Harvey more gently, even when he is wrong. Able, brainy fellow and one of my boys. A little joke now and then all right, but don't handle him too severely. I like him."

In late 1907, Pulitzer's new ship was ready. He christened it *Liberty* to signify the hopes he had for how it would change his life. He hoped that the ship would bring him freedom from the frustrations that unnerved him. The almost all-white ship, valued at about $1,500,000, was 270 feet long. It had a huge cabin with thick carpeting, double doors and portholes, and a four-poster bed. A crew of sixty ran the ship; other staff increased the maintenance total to seventy-five. His bedroom was lined with books. His sink was extra-high so he would not have to stoop. A set of electric bells hung over his bed, labeled so that he could easily call his steward, the captain, or a secretary. He had almost complete control of all the people on the ship. Because they were all on the ship, they could not ignore his calls.

In the 1908 presidential election, Pulitzer found it hard to support either major candidate. He did not agree with the economic policies of Democratic candidate William Jennings Bryan. However, his own

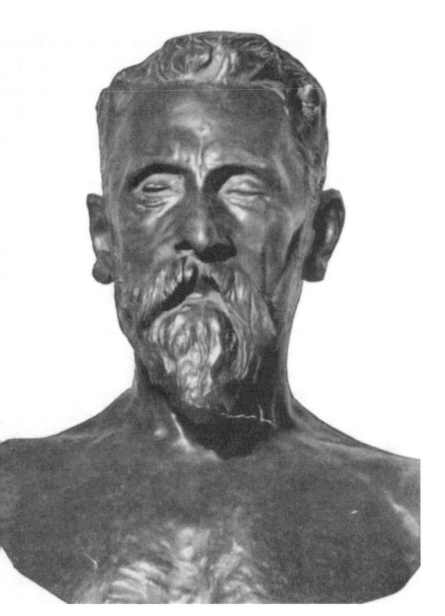

Pulitzer quarreled with the famous sculptor Auguste Rodin while posing for this bust.

sympathies and those of the *World* had long sided with the Democrats. He did not want to support Republican Howard Taft.

Now a story that had begun seven years earlier came back to haunt him. In 1901, President Theodore Roosevelt had opened negotiations with both Panama and Nicaragua about building a canal in one of these countries. In 1903, Panama granted the rights for the canal to the United States. Over the years, reports surfaced about conspiracy and misappropriation of funds in connection with the matter. In 1908, the *World* called for a congressional investigation of "President Roosevelt's deliberate misstatements of fact."

Roosevelt answered that the stories in the *World* were libelous and false in every detail. He added: "the attorney general has under consideration the form in which the proceedings against Mr. Pulitzer shall be brought." Pulitzer had his headline almost immediately— "Mr. Roosevelt is mistaken. He cannot muzzle the *World.*"

While waiting for Roosevelt's response, Pulitzer sailed for the West Indies. The case of Roosevelt vs. Pulitzer continued both in fact and in rumor. Indictments, a summons, and bench warrants were drawn up in District Criminal Court #1.

From his ship, Pulitzer continued to encourage Cobb to write editorials condemning Roosevelt and condemning censorship of the press. He labeled Roosevelt as "drunk with success, drunk with power, drunk with popularity."

In mid-March, Pulitzer sailed for Lisbon, Portugal. The weather was terrible, the gales were high, and Pulitzer suffered from a bronchial infection. The *Liberty* finally made shore, and a doctor diagnosed Pulitzer's problem as potentially deadly. Pulitzer had whooping cough, and at his age and condition, this could kill him. Pulitzer traveled to Marseilles where rest and the weather cured him.

In July 1908, Pulitzer visited the office building for the second time in eighteen years. He came to see the new addition. He complained about the furniture arrangement and asked reporters about their work. He left, upset about what he had found.

Pulitzer named his steam yacht Liberty because it was supposed to make him free from the frustrations that made his daily life miserable.

That August he sailed out of the country, sure that he could not stand the excitement of the fall election. An immediate problem was to hire a doctor to take the place of his retiring doctor and companion. He interviewed and rejected a long list of candidates—one had not read widely enough, another ate too noisily, another wore perfume, and so on. Although suffering from insomnia, indigestion, and headaches, he found energy to pay attention to his son, Herbert. He believed that Herbert might make up for the disappointments he felt with Ralph and Joseph. He desperately needed someone to love, and Herbert was the almost perfect candidate. Pulitzer created a pressing schedule for him—German lessons both in conversation and writing, formal dinners, operas, and tennis.

In the fall of 1908, Pulitzer returned to the States to await the elections. He gave explicit orders to the editor-in-chief that the *World* was not to praise candidate Republican William Taft when he won except as necessary to acknowledge his victory. Taft won by over a million votes. Pulitzer ordered his staff to make sure they treated the new president with fairness and honesty.

Pulitzer changed the will he had drawn up in 1904. In the new division of assets of the publishing company, he left sixty percent to Herbert, twenty per cent to Ralph, ten per cent to Joseph, and the rest to major editors and managers. He left instructions that all his sons and their descendants accept "the duty of preserving, perfecting, and perpetuating *The World* newspaper in the same spirit in which I have striven to create and conduct it as a public institution, from motives higher than mere gain." He left nothing to his daughters, fearing that they might be the victims of fortune hunters.

Pulitzer worried about his heart. He said, "Real troubles never bother me. It's only the small annoyances that upset me. I am no longer equal to thinking or deciding." He said he had received warnings that he would not live long.

Despite Pulitzer's health problems, he tried to take control of Ralph's every move. Kate begged Pulitzer to take it easy on his son: "In the future should Ralph not come up to your expectations in some things or dissatisfy you in others, remember that you cannot make a man to please yourself, but let the man make himself even though his way might not be your way."

Chapter Nine

In a World of His Own

After eight years of training with his father, Ralph still did not have the competitive spirit that his father felt was necessary to success. Hoping that a rise in status might achieve the desired attitude, Pulitzer elevated his son to vice president of the paper. Soon after he received the new title, Ralph went on a two-week vacation to Canada. Because of bad weather, he could not return to New York on time. When he did get there, he found a note from his father asking for his resignation. Ralph sent the resignation.

The matter did not end there. Ralph needed the job for the money. He wrote to his father, describing the travel problems that had kept him from getting to New York. He reminded him that he, like his father, suffered from physical problems. He said that he had to have the money in order to care for his family. Pulitzer's answer was to restore the salary, but not the title of vice president.

Pulitzer was exhausted from the whooping cough, the strain of the court case, his family problems, and his worries about the newspaper. He stayed abroad throughout 1909, traveling in Norway, France, and Germany. Every apartment he stayed in was specially prepared for him to block out sound. The thickest possible glass was added to windows in his apartment. The floors were covered with heavy carpets. Windows and doors were hung with heavy curtains.

Still, there was no way to totally soundproof his life. One of

Pulitzer's secretaries, Alleyne Ireland, wrote a book, *Adventures with a Genius*, about his relationship with Pulitzer. He described Pulitzer: "a very tall man with broad shoulders tapering away to thinness One eye was dull and half closed, the other was of a deep, brilliant blue." Ireland described the pre-job interview with Pulitzer. Pulitzer told him "I must explore your brain, your character, your tastes your sympathies, your prejudices, your temper; I must find out if you have tact, patience, a sense of humor, the gift of condensing information, and, above all, a respect, a love, a passion for accuracy." Ireland reported that the click of a spoon against a saucer or the striking of a match could make Pulitzer weak. He said he saw his employer break into perspiration and turn pale at these sounds.

In October, Pulitzer's brother Albert committed suicide. This was especially distressing to Pulitzer because he had watched his brother's mental derangement increase. He could only wonder if the same fate was in store for him.

That same month, Roosevelt's case against the *World* was dismissed in Indianapolis federal court. The conclusion was that no one would ever know the full truth about the Panama situation. Pulitzer might have let the case drop there and savored his victory. But he would not. He insisted on continuing the part of the case that dealt with freedom of the press. He wanted to establish the precedent that the government could not challenge the freedom of the press as Roosevelt had.

In December, Pulitzer frequently sailed on the *Liberty* to Corsica, Monte Carlo, and Elba. He spent the winter of 1909-1910 at Cape Martin. He was now almost totally blind. He no longer used a strong electric lamp at dinner to show him his food; it would do no good. When a friend tried to show him a particularly beautiful sunset from the boat, he said, "It's no use, my dear boy, I cannot even get a glimmer of its light."

He continued to search for a doctor who could ease his suffering.

Pulitzer, almost totally blind, spent the winter of 1910 on the French coast.

He saw many famous practitioners in Europe, spent a lot of money, and found out nothing new. His closest friends looked on this doctor-seeking as more of a hobby than a hope. He asked his secretary to find a doctor to accompany him for a month to Turkey, Greece, and Egypt. This time, he did not insist that the doctor also be a companion. That doctor's sole purpose would be to study and diagnose Pulitzer's problems. Pulitzer thought he found the practitioner he was looking for, and he summoned the man. When the doctor arrived, he was told that Pulitzer was too sick to see him.

He continued to write long letters of instructions to editorial writers at the *World*. In one letter he seemed to give up a little control over his editors. He wrote: "I do not wish to kill initiative, courage, discretion in the gentleman who is in charge of the page." In other letters, he sent detailed instructions on issues, past practices, and the attitude of the *World* toward specific people and projects.

In a bulletin to a managing editor, he discussed three goals of the paper: one was to be talked about, one was to be prepared to write an important story each day, one was to make a paper readable for every class of society. He said about the editorial page: "It lacks persistence and continuing force. Instead of striking once, it should strike a dozen times; hammer its ideas into the people's...heads the *World* should be more powerful than the President."

In January of 1911, Pulitzer finally received a decision from the Supreme Court on his suit against the government concerning freedom of the press. The unanimous decision declared that the government could not obstruct the freedom of the press. The justices added that they hoped that presidents from that time on would heed the lesson taught to Theodore Roosevelt.

Pulitzer developed a daily routine. A typical day would begin with breakfast during which he was read articles from magazines, previewed and condensed ahead of time. Then he sat alone with his closest confidante and dictated especially private letters. Then he made his plans for the day. Sometimes he went for an automobile ride. He loved what he called speed—sometimes eighty km (a little under fifty miles) an hour. The sightless man often dictated letters as he rode. Next came a secretary who read from papers published in America, London, and Paris. This secretary was expected to point out the differences in coverage of certain articles by the *World* and other New York papers. Then he called in another secretary and dictated his notes, comments, and replies to the articles he had just heard. Then came another secretary whose job was to create and maintain stimulating conversation. Then he had a twenty minute stroll with another secretary who summarized for him articles from half a dozen or so magazines. In his book, Ireland wrote that Pulitzer asked him to summarize articles on composer Richard Wagner, justice in England and the United States, New Zealand, lawyers, tariffs, the Smithsonian Institute, the Panama Canal, the Declaration of Independence, the German government, American trade, and polygamy—all in one hour.

After lunch with all of his secretaries, Pulitzer was read to sleep by another secretary. When he awoke, Pulitzer went back to listening to newspaper articles and dictating letters. During dinner, a secretary might be asked to discuss any number of different topics—a certain scene of a play, the British Parliament, the government of ancient Athens. Each secretary was supposed to be ready to discuss intellectually any topic that happened to be on Pulitzer's mind at the time.

After dinner he sometimes attended a concert or heard one secretary read from a play while another played the piano. Ireland wrote about how hard it was to read steadily while just ten feet away a piano player worked on a repertoire sometimes soft, sometimes rousing, sometimes grave and deep. When Pulitzer began to feel sleepy, usually around nine o'clock, he retired to his bedroom where a secretary would read to him until he fell asleep. He was never alone for a moment except when he was asleep.

He could not bear to visit with his children and grandchildren either frequently or for long visits. He believed that their failures completely unnerved him, and that he was always weaker after visiting with them.

He complained that politics left him with the same sick feelings that his family did. But he was able to overcome this nervous problem more easily with politics than with his family. He scored a political victory in his quest to get President Taft and the Congress to enact tax relief. Pulitzer sent questionnaires to prominent people, asking their opinion. He sent these answers, most of them positive, to Congress. A special session of Congress enacted a reduction in tariffs.

He protested against women getting the vote. He gave his editors an idea about how to fight against it: "Analyze, argue against it without fear women worship might at least be subjected to truth."

In all his interactions with others, he presented a problem. No one knew what his mood would be. He bounced from optimism to pessimism, from control to paranoia, from a feeling of success to a feeling of failure, from hopefulness about his health to a fear of dying at any minute, from weariness to a spurt of energy. People who loved him or felt it necessary to communicate with him learned to judge these moods and to act accordingly.

These contradictions displayed themselves in more than his emotions. They also ruled his actions. Sometimes he fled from responsibility, pleading illness. At other times he demanded action. He tried to explain these attitudes to himself: "I hate the idea of passing away known only as the proprietor of the paper. Not property, but politics was my passion, and not politics in the general, selfish sense, but politics in the sense of liberty, freedom and ideals of justice."

He commissioned portrait artist John Sargent to paint his picture. He told him, "I want to be remembered just as I really am, with all my strain and suffering there."

In the fall of 1911, Pulitzer sailed on the *Liberty*, hoping that the company of his youngest son, Herbert, would bring him peace. On the second day out, he did not feel well. He did not want to trust the diagnosis of the doctor on board. So they put into Charleston, South Carolina to see another doctor. That doctor said that he had a case of indigestion, and he prescribed medicine accordingly.

On Sunday October 29, Pulitzer was lethargic, sleepy and often whispered "softly, quite softly." Mrs. Pulitzer was called. He died at twenty until two. The cause of his death was listed as heart failure. In his will, he left $1.5 million to Columbia's Graduate School of Journalism and $500,000 to endow the first national awards for books, drama, music, and journalism. William Randolph Hearst wrote of him: "A towering figure from national and international journalism has passed away; a mighty democratic force in the life of the nation and in the activity of the world has ceased; a great power uniformly exerted in behalf of popular rights and human progress is ended. Joseph Pulitzer is dead."

Chapter Ten

The *World* Without Joseph Pulitzer, Sr.

At their father's death, Joseph took total responsibility for the *Post-Dispatch*, and Ralph took over the *World*. Although Herbert was officially listed as working with Ralph, he showed little or no interest, and he seldom came into the *World* offices.

Through the 1920s it became obvious that the *World*, called the *Evening World,* was not meeting its competition. Probable causes were poor reporting and lack of strong news policy.

By the mid 1920s three tabloids, including Hearst's *Mirror*, were strong competitors both for readers and for advertisers.

The owner of the *Telegram* and the *Sun* offered to buy the *Evening World* for five million. Joseph and Ralph considered the sale. Joseph was enthusiastic, although the *World* was not his paper. He believed that the *Evening World* had become simply a lightweight paper focusing on crime and gossip. He thought it would be good strategy to get rid of the *Evening World* so they could concentrate on the *Morning* and *Sunday World*. Ralph did not agree. He thought that selling the *Evening World* would signal defeat for the Pulitzers. He also thought that they could get much more than five million if they simply waited.

Before either brother could take any direct action, Ralph received orders from his doctor to stop working immediately, or risk a nervous breakdown. He turned over the presidency to Herbert and left the country.

In April, a representative from the *New York Times* asked Herbert if the *New York World* was for sale. The two men talked but came to no agreement. The economy of the country slid into a full-scale depression with heavy unemployment and low profits. Near the end of 1930, Roy Howard of the Scripps-Howard newspaper chain offered five million for all three papers, the *Evening World,* the *Sunday World,* and the *World*. This seemed like a wonderful opportunity until the brothers checked the will. Pulitzer had stipulated that each paper had to be handled separately; there could be no agreement about one paper without consideration of all three at the same time. The brothers went to court to see if they could break their father's will. They were successful. Scripps-Howard bought the papers for $5,000,000.

Joseph Pulitzer was a complicated man. He was a spokeman for the poor who sometimes manipulated readers for his own political ends. A victim of poor health his entire life, he was also a man of extraordinary energy. He would do almost anything to incease circulation at his paper, but was also deeply concerned about his adopted country.

Pulitzer's legacy in American journalism remains strong. Today he is best remembered for his establishment of the Pulitzer Prizes and his endowment of the Columbia School of Journalism, probably the most highly respected journalism school in the world. His influence is more powerful. He taught journalists that they needed to do more than write—they also had to attract readers. He showed politicians and business leaders that they had to respond to their constituents and customers. He taught the poor and less powerful that they should be interested in the public affairs of their community and country—to do more than complain.

Joseph Pulitzer left a huge, sometimes conflicting legacy. One point is certain, however. Readers, viewers, and citizens will be dealing with these issues for many years to come.

Timeline

1847—born in Mako, Hungary
1864—immigrated to the United States
1864—joined Union army
1867—became an American citizen
1871—became managing editor of the *Westliche Post*
1869—elected to the Missouri House of Representatives
1878—bought the *St. Louis Dispatch*
1883—bought the *New York World*
1898—called a yellow journalist for his coverage of the Spanish-
   American War
1911—died in Charleston, South Carolina

Appendix
Pulitzer's Advice to His Writers

1. Be accurate.
2. Be concise.
3. Never write about a trivial topic.
4. Be absolutely fair.
5. Write about concrete current topics, never about abstractions.
6. Wherever possible, use facts, figures, and statistics.
7. Rise above partisanship and popular prejudice.
8. Do not talk about public people in private.
9. Use word pictures to describe events so that readers feel as though they were on the scene.
10. Make your opening sentence and paragraph particularly striking.
11. Use history when possible to make an argument stronger.
12. Book reviewers should state first the most interesting points of the book, then the focus of the book, then—if there is room, the reviewer's opinion.

Questions and Answers About the Pulitzer Prizes

WHAT PRIZES DID PULITZER SPECIFY?
He specified nine prizes—four in journalism, three in literature, one in drama, and one in essay writing. After his death, more prizes were awarded to include poetry and music prizes and ten more journalistic awards including photography, criticism, and commentary.

WHEN WAS THE FIRST AWARD GIVEN?
The first awards were made in 1917.

ARE THERE ANY REQUIREMENTS FOR ENTERING THE COMPETITION?
Yes, the entrance fee is $20 and a candidate must submit four copies of the work. A candidate for the music prize must submit a recording.

HOW ARE THE WINNERS CHOSEN?
Eighty-six men and women, called juries, work on screening committees that nominate a list of finalists for each prize. These nominations are approved or disapproved by a smaller Advisory Board. The approved names are passed on to a board of sixteen men and women called the Pulitzer Prize Board, which makes the final selections.

WHERE ARE THE AWARDS PRESENTED?
The prizes are announced in the World Room (named after Pulitzer's *World*), a large lecture hall in Columbia's Graduate School of Journalism.

IS THERE ANY CONTROVERSY ABOUT THE SELECTION OF PRIZE WINNERS?

Yes. Every year except two, the board has overturned at least one jury recommendation. Also, every year one or more decisions by the Pulitzer Prize Board creates controversy among publishers and writers. Sometimes the controversy is about accuracy, sometimes about alleged facts.

HOW MUCH MONEY IS AWARDED TO EACH WINNER?

Each prize carries a $3,000 award.

DO PULITZER PRIZE WINNERS RECEIVE A MEDAL?

No. A gold meal is awarded to a newspaper each year, never to an individual.

HOW DO THE AWARDS AFFECT THOSE WHO WIN?

Journalists who win a Pulitzer Prize can expect better job openings and improved assignments and better working arrangements where they work. Publishers of Pulitzer-award winning work often experience increased readership and a reputation which attracts more top talent to the staff. Award-winning book authors experience increased sales and often more lucrative contracts for their next work. Poets may receive travel stipends and increased fees for readings. Musicians may receive commissions for their work.

WHEN DO WINNERS LEARN THAT THEY HAVE WON?

Members of the screening committee are asked to keep their nominations secret. However, usually one or another member fails to keep the secrecy. Nominated persons usually know who they are before the award-winning ceremony; they do not know who the grand prize winners are until the announcements are made.

DOES EACH CLASSIFICATION WIN AN AWARD EACH YEAR?

No. Sometimes the selection committee finds no nomination worthy. In 1941 and 1974, no award was given in the novel category. In 1947 and 1986, the Board did not award a prize for drama. In 1965, no Pulitzer was awarded for music, but a citation was awarded to jazz band leader Duke Ellington.

HAS AN AWARD EVER BEEN REVOKED?

Yes, in 1981, the Pulitzer Prize for a feature story was awarded to

Washington Post writer Janet Cooke. The award was taken away when it was discovered that Cooke had made up her feature story about an eight-year-old heroin addict.

DID ANYONE EVER REFUSE A PULITZER PRIZE?

Yes, in 1926 novelist Sinclair Lewis rejected the prize, saying that "seekers for prizes tend to labor not for inherent excellence but for alien rewards" (However Lewis did accept a Pulitzer Prize in 1930.) In 1940, playwright William Saroyan refused the award, for *The Time of Your Life*, saying that a Pulitzer Prize was a "consecration of the mediocre."

WHAT WELL-KNOWN FICTION HAS RECEIVED A PULITZER PRIZE?

Among the arts/fiction winners are

(1926) *Arrowsmith* by Sinclair Lewis
(1932) *The Good Earth* by Pearl Buck
(1937) *Gone with the Wind* by Margaret Mitchell
(1939) *The Yearling* by Marjorie Kinnan Rawlings
(1940) *The Grapes of Wrath* by John Steinbeck
(1953) *The Old Man and the Sea* by Ernest Hemingway
(1961) *To Kill a Mockingbird* by Harper Lee
(1983) *The Color Purple* by Alice Walker
(1991) *Beloved* by Toni Morrison
(1995) *The Stone Diaries* by Carol Shields
(1998) *American Pastoral* by Philip Roth

WHAT ARE SOME REASONS WHY SPECIAL CITATIONS WERE AWARDED?

Defense of freedom (*Edmonton Journal*)
Efforts to advance Pulitzer Prizes (Columbia University School of Journalism)
Exposition of corruption in college basketball (*New York Journal-American*)
Service on the Pulitzer Board (Joseph Pulitzer, Jr.)

Bibliography

Bates, Douglas. *Pulitzer Prizes*. New York: A Birch Lane Press Book, 1991.

Desmond, Robert. *The Information Process: World News Reporting to the Twentieth Century*. Iowa: University of Iowa Press, 1978.

Heaton, John. *The Story of a Page*. New York: Harper & Brothers Publishers, 1913.

Hohenberg, John. *The Pulitzer Prizes*. New York: Columbia University Press, 1974.

Juergens, Geroge. *Joseph Pulitzer and the New York World*. New Jersey: Princeton University Press, 1966.

Pfaff, Daniel. *Joseph Pulitzer II and the Post-Dispatch*. Pennsylvania: The Pennsylvania State University Press, 1991.

Seitz, Don. *Joseph Pulitzer: His Life and Letters*. New York: Garden City Publishing Co., Inc., 1924.

Schwartz, Bernard. *The Law in America*. New York: McGraw-Hill Book Company, 1974.

Swanberg, W. A. *Pulitzer*. New York: Charles Scribner's Sons, 1967.

Sources

CHAPTER ONE

p.11, "Take that little ----" Seitz, Don. *Joseph Pulitzer.* New York: Garden City, 1927

p.13, "good moral character," Schwartz, Bernard. The *Law in America.* New York: McGraw-Hill Book Company, 1974, p.78

p.15, "I, the unknown, the luckless," Seitz, op.cit., p.58

p.15, "He was quick, intelligent and enthusiastic," Seitz, op.cit., p.61

CHAPTER TWO

p.20, "We are one people," Seitz, op.cit., p.89

p.21, "I cannot help saying," Swanberg, W. A. *Pulitzer.* New York: Charles Scribner's Sons, 1967, p.39

p.21, "become worthy of you," Seitz, op.cit., p.92

p.21, "Write me every day," Seitz, op.cit., p.94

p.24, "The *Post and Dispatch* will serve no party," Seitz, op.cit., p.101

p.24, "What is the great demoralizer," Swanberg, op.cit., p.48

p.27, "but some day I am going," Swanberg, op.cit., p.54

p.27, "I am out of public life," Swanberg, op.cit., p.15

p.28, "An Adulterous Pair, Duped," Swanberg, op.cit., p.59

CHAPTER THREE

p.31, "If there is anything in my melancholy," Seitz, op.cit., p.132

p.32, "Heretofore you have all been living," Swanberg, op.cit., p.70

p.35, "If you had asked a man." Juergens, George. *Joseph Pulitzer and the New York World.* Princeton: Princeton University Press, 1966

CHAPTER FOUR

p.37, "he is an honest man," Swanberg, op.cit., p.82

p.38, "Let those who are startled," Juergens, op.cit., p.70

p.41,"Money must be raised to complete," Seitz, op.cit., p.156

p.41,"lonely and very aged woman," Seitz, op.cit, p.157

p.42,"Accuracy! Accuracy! Accuracy!" Swanberg, op. cit., p.127

p.43,"He must never go home," Swanberg, op.cit., p.76

p.43"[He said] I did not understand," Swanberg, op.cit., p.112

p.43 "Mr. Pulitzer has no friends," Seitz, op.cit., p.18

p.46 "The Jew who does not want," Swanberg, op.cit., p.146

p. 46 "Move on, Pulitzer," Swanberg, op.cit., p.147

p.49 "Even the shabby little building," Swanberg, op.cit., p.149

p.49 "It is well done." Swanberg, op.cit., p.154

p.49 "God grant that this structure," Seitz, op.cit., p.171

p.49 "whenever anything went wrong," Swanberg, op.cit., p.151

p.52 "It's dark to me." Seitz, op.cit., p.177

p.52 "[he] passed days on a sofa," Swanberg, op.cit., p.159

p.52 "Yielding to the advice," Seitz, op.cit., p.179

p.53 "I can conscientiously say," Pfaff, Daniel. *Joseph Pulitzer II and the Post-Dispatch.* Pennsylvania: The Pennsylvania State University Press, 1991, p.23

p.53 "I really feel that," Pfaff, Daniel. op.cit., p.24

p.53 "A man with a most astonishing range," Swanberg, op.cit., p.208

p.56 "I am the loneliest man," Swanberg, op.cit., p.192

CHAPTER SIX

p.57 "As long as I find fault," Swanberg, op.cit., p.177

p.60 "don't you think you should have," Pfaff, op.cit., p.21

p.60 "To interfere in South America," Seitz, op.cit., p.203

p.62 "Let the war once dominate," Seitz, op.cit., p. 204

p.62 " It [the dispute] is not our frontier." Swanberg, op.cit., p.198

p.62 "publicity had done its work" Seitz, op.cit., p.206

p.65 "Sound the cymbals" Seitz, op.cit., p.254

CHAPTER SEVEN

p.69 "Blood on the roadsides" Swanberg, op.cit., p.227

p.70 "I want a radical reduction" Swanberg, op.cit., p.231

p.72 "that naturally meant that the books" Pfaff, op.cit., p.21

p.73 "The entire Spanish fleet of eleven vessels" Seitz, op.cit., p.240

p.74 "What are the Philippines?" Seitz, op.cit., p.243

p.76 "I ask was there ever a human being" Swanberg, op.cit., p.288

p.76 " the least you could have done" Pfaff, op.cit., p.27

p.76 "You should consider yourself very fortunate" Swanberg, op.cit., p.289

CHAPTER EIGHT

p.79 "You must try to write as little" Seitz, op.cit., p.257

p.79 "they present a very good example" Seitz, op.cit., p.259

p.80 "you could not possibly please me" Seitz, op.cit., p.280

p.80 "too dry, too melancholy, too much corruption" Seitz, op.cit., p.274

p.82 "I think I have, so far," Pfaff, op.cit., p.169

p.84 "I love this boat," Seitz, op.cit., p.290

p.84 "you would be so much happier" Swanberg, op.cit., p.337

p.84 "I want some love and affection" Pfaff, op. Cit., p.81

p.85 "I might send you an order" Seitz, op.cit., p.36

p.86 "Tell Cobb, Seymour, etc. to treat" Seitz, op.cit., p.30

p.88 "President Roosevelt's deliberate" Swanberg, op.cit., p.366

p.88 "The Attorney General has under consideration" Swanberg, op.cit., p.368.

p.88 "Mr. Roosevelt is mistaken" Swanberg, ibid.

p.88 "drunk with success" Seitz, op.cit., p.72

p.90 "the duty of preserving, perfecting," Pfaff, op.cit., p.101

p. 90 "Real troubles never bother" Seitz, op.cit., p.392-3

p.90 "In the future should Ralph" Swanberg, op.cit., p.354

CHAPTER NINE

p.92 "a very tall man" Ireland, Alleyne. *Reminiscences of a Secretary* (also published as *Adventures with a Genius*). New York: Mitchell Kennerley, 1914, p.39

p.92 "I must explore" Ireland, op.cit., p.62

p.92 "It's no use, my dear boy" Seitz, op.cit., p.392

p.94 "I do not wish to kill initiative" Seitz, op.cit., p.402

p.94 "It lacks persistence" Seitz, op.cit., p.406

p.96 "Analyze, argue against it" Seitz, op.cit., p.410

p.96 "I hate the idea of passing away" Seitz, op.cit., p.xiv

p.96 "I want to be remembered" Ibid.

p.97 "softly, quite softly" Seitz, op.cit., p.415

p.97 "A towering figure from national" Swanberg, op.cit., p.412

Index